FROM THE GREAT DEPRESSION TO WORLD WAR II

JOSEPH SZALAY

TURNER PUBLISHING COMPANY

TURNER PUBLISHING COMPANY
412 Broadway • P.O. Box 3101
Paducah, Kentucky   42002-3101
(270) 443-0121

Turner Publishing Company Staff:
Editor: Dayna Spear Williams
Designer: Peter Zuniga

Library of Congress Catalog Card No.
2001099207

ISBN: 978-1-68162-342-9

Additional copies may be purchased directly from the publisher.
Limited Edition.

FROM THE GREAT DEPRESSION TO WORLD WAR II

Joseph J. Szalay

DEDICATION

This book is dedicated to our daughter, Carolyn Nolan and our son, James "Butch" Szalay. Our son and I spent many days together camping at Platt National Park near Sulphur, OK. We also camped out at Galveston near the water's edge. We enjoyed eating at the wonderful restaurants along the sea-wall. Our son died of a heart attack March 1996. He was only 48 years old.

Daughter
Carolyn Jo Nolan

Our daughter was a joy to be with. We looked forward to her visits several times a month. When she arrived at our back door, she gave us that smile that all was well with the world. She loved life and enjoyed every moment until she was struck down by a terrible cancer that took her life at age 55, March 1999. She gave us two fine grandsons that give us all the love that we can handle.

We miss both of our children very much but life goes on and we must accept these facts and make the best of these circumstances.

Son
James "Butch" Szalay

ACKNOWLEDGMENTS

I wish to thank Mr. Don Eldridge, editor at the *Herald Democrat* in Sherman, TX for his continued interest in publishing these articles in the local newspaper from December 1991 to October 2001.

I also want to thank my wife, Marie, for the hours spent typing these stories the past several years. Thanks also to my grandson's wife, Lea Nolan, for helping out with the typing on several occasions. My thanks also to Venita Johnson for typing numerous articles the past several months. My sincere thanks to Willis Hastings for his encouragement for me to continue writing these stories.

✜ ——•——•—— ✜

TELLING MY STORIES

Professor Jerry Lincecum, an instructor at Austin College in Sherman, TX started a program a few years ago called "Telling Our Stories."

The classes met on Sunday afternoons for several months each year. It was intended to interest senior citizens to tell stories of their experiences, in writing, for their families, children and grandchildren.

Willis Hastings, an acquaintance of mine, wrote an article about his experience as a bombardier during WWII. His plane was shot down and he parachuted out of his plane and landed in Hungary. He became a prisoner of war near the town of Miscolc, Hungary and was eventually taken to prison camps in Germany.

My parents were born in Hungary and I remember them mentioning the town of Miscolc on several occasions. I visited with Willis Hastings and told him that I remember some stories that my parents talked about this town. He suggested that I write an article about my parents' birthplace in Hungary and their experiences growing up working on farms that were owned by wealthy landowners.

I wrote an article as suggested by Willis and had him read it and make some comments. He told me to take it to the local newspaper, *The Herald Democrat* and talk to Don Eldridge, the editor. Apparently, the editor felt that the article had merit and it was published in the next Sunday edition.

The editor's approval increased my interest in writing and I started to write articles that were published about once a month. This has been going on for over 10 years and I still enjoy writing.

My friends told me that I had a special talent and that I should put these articles in a book. This book is the result of all the encouragement I got from many of my friends who enjoyed my articles the past few years.

BIRTHPLACE MEMORIES

I was born January 3, 1919 in Duquesne, PA. My parents came to America about the turn of the century when immigration was at its peak. They were processed through Ellis Island with thousands of immigrants who came from various countries of Europe, Africa and Asia.

My parents came from Agad, Zemplain County of Hungary. They met in Duquesne and got married about 1900. They lived there all their lives.

My father worked at the Carnegie-Illinois Steel Mills in Duquesne most of his adult life and retired at age 65. Mother died at age 33 and my father tried to take care of our family of two boys and four girls. A year or so later he placed a brother and two sisters in an orphanage since he was unable to care for all of us and continue to work in the steel mills. The two older sisters went to live with friends and I went to live with my Aunt Mary.

After the stock market crash in 1929, which was the beginning of the great depression, I worked for local grocery stores, fruit and vegetable stores and other places from age 10 for $2.50 a week. I continued working at these places until I graduated from high school in 1936. During the summer I worked at Kennywood Amusement Park, from age 15 to 17 for 25 cents an hour. I worked about 70 hours a week and made $17 to $20 a week.

After graduation from Duquesne High School in 1936, I joined the Civilian Conservation Corps and stayed there for one year. We did soil conservation work which included building small earth dams.

In 1938, I went to work in the steel mills as a laborer and about a year later I worked as an apprentice in the forge shop. I earned 50 cents an hour which was the going rate for this type of work. I left this job in 1941 when I was drafted into military service.

The military service was for one year but this was extended 18 months when the world situation demanded more drastic measures. After Pearl Harbor on December 7, 1941 the term of service was extended for the duration. I served overseas from September 1944 until December 1945 and was discharged in March 1946. Our unit was in combat in Germany from November 1944 until May 1945. After the war, we served in the Army of Occupation until December 1945, at which time we sailed from Europe back to the good old USA.

While in the service I married Marie James of Paris, TX in April 1943. When I returned from service I settled in Paris, TX and went to work for Texas Power and Light Company. I worked there for 35 years and retired in 1981. We raised two beautiful children who died at a very young age. Our daughter died of cancer at the age of 55 and our son died at the age of 48 of a heart attack.

MILITARY SERVICE

I was drafted into military service January 18, 1941. I was sent to Fort Meade, MD for processing which included taking a battery of tests that lasted three days. These tests were used to determine your special skills and aptitude that would determine your military assignment.

Our entire group was sent to Dodd Field, Fort Sam Houston, TX for basic training. After eight weeks of basic training, we were assigned to Company B, 23rd Infantry Regiment, 2nd Infantry Division. The test results apparently had little effect on our assignment to the infantry.

I received infantry training from March 1941 until about March 1942. At this time I applied for a transfer to the military language school because of my knowledge of the Hungarian language. My application was approved by my company commander who forwarded it to the Division G-2, which was the military intelligence organization of the 2nd Infantry Division. The officer in charge of the Division G-2 section interviewed me and advised me that I would be given tests to determine my aptitude for this military duty. After the tests, which I passed, I was advised that a vacancy would be available for me to be assigned to the G-2 section of a new division.

I was placed in charge of training the personnel that would be assigned to the G-2 section of the new division. I was given field manuals and scheduled to start the training immediately.

I was promoted to corporal and taught classes on military intelligence for several weeks. The cadre for the new division, the

102nd Infantry Division, was being organized and prepared to leave the 2nd Infantry Division in the near future.

In June 1942, the cadre was sent to Camp Swift near Austin, TX to continue our training until the 102nd Infantry Division Camp was ready. In August 1942, we were ordered to proceed to Camp Maxey, Paris, TX to the 102nd Infantry Division Camp which was nearing completion. Our Division Headquarters office and barracks were just about ready for occupancy. We had to use an outdoor privy for a couple of days until all the plumbing was completed.

I was charged with the responsibility to continue training the G-2 section for the next several months. In the meantime, I was promoted to sergeant, staff sergeant and finally master sergeant.

Lt. Colonel Thayer was in charge of the G-2 section and he was a very strict disciplinarian. Since the camp was new, there were several things that we needed that were not available. Col. Thayer would not accept that fact and he advised me to improvise. I made numerous trips to various buildings in the camp looking for material to improvise with to satisfy Col. Thayer.

In December 1942, we received word that there would be warrant officer vacancies available and applications should be submitted to the Division Adjutant General's office. I applied and was scheduled for an interview and exam in the near future. I spent the next several days studying and preparing for this opportunity. I burned the midnight oil reading and memorizing Army regulations and other military subjects.

The day for my interview and exam finally came. I was seated in a chair in front of a group of staff officers from the Division Headquarters. There were six officers of various ranks to include a couple of majors and lieutenant colonels. I was quizzed for a couple of hours (more or less) regarding military procedures and Army regulations. Fortunately, I studied the right subjects and Army regulations and apparently passed all questions to the satisfaction of the officers in charge of the interview and exam.

A few days later, I was officially notified that I passed the exams and was appointed warrant officer junior grade. I was assigned to the 380th FA Battalion as personnel officer.

I was greeted by Lt. Col. Hannigan, commander of the 380th FA Battalion and was told that he was very proud to have me assigned to his organization. Col. Hannigan was a West Point graduate and a very fine military officer. He was a fine person to work for and I enjoyed being a member of his organization. After a year of serving as his personnel officer, I was promoted to chief warrant officer.

Brand New Recruits
With buddy, George Kocak, at Fort Sam Houston, 1941.

I served under his command during the remainder of my tour of military duty and 16 months overseas in Europe which included combat duty in Germany.

THE GREAT DEPRESSION

THOUGHTS OF OLD COUNTRY REVIVED
Sunday, December 1, 1991

The article in the *Sherman Democrat* dated Nov. 10, 1991 by Willis Hastings prompted me to write this. He mentioned the town of Miscolc, Hungary, which caught my eye.

My parents were born in Hungary in a small village named Agad, in the county of Zemplane. I remember them talking about the city of Miscolc, which apparently was the nearest city of any size from their village.

Life in these villages in Hungary were similar to life years ago when large landowners ruled the kingdom. Everyone worked in the fields for these wealthy landowners. Oxen were the beast of burden in most of Europe before the turn of the century. Back-breaking work in the fields was the order of the day from pre-school age to adult age and beyond.

America offered hope and people from the Old Country dreamed of one day coming to the land of milk and honey. Since my mother died when I was only 13 years old and since dad could not take care of the three younger sisters and brother, they were placed in an orphanage. I went to live with my Aunt Mary and the opportunity to learn more about my roots was the least of my worries.

Dad was about 15 years old when he came to America and mother was probably the same age. I remember dad told us that they came through a terrible storm in the Atlantic and all the boys and men had to help pump the water out of the boat to keep it from sinking.

I was never able to find out who sponsored my parents' trip from the Old Country since dad died before I was interested enough to learn more about our family history. It's possible that some wealthy landowner may have sponsored many of the villagers since they expected to be paid handsomely for providing the funds to make the trip to America.

Everyone coming to America expected to get rich in a short time and to return to the Old Country and live like a king. It didn't happen that way and very few people ever had the means to return to the homeland. I remember dad had mentioned to us many times when we were young that he would take us back to the Old Country.

Well, it never did happen. There were a lot of lean years and then the Great Depression that ended all hope of making the trip.

Although my parents were born in the same village, I don't believe they knew each other until they met in America. My parents apparently married about 1890-1900. They came through Ellis Island, which was the gateway to America for thousands of immigrants.

Dad and mother somehow made their way to Duquesne, PA (10 miles south of Pittsburgh) where dad went to work in the steel mills. Mother went to work for some wealthy businessman in Squirrel Hill (all the elite of Pittsburgh lived there) as a cook and housekeeper. Apparently they were married after they both had secured employment.

Several months ago I read an article in a magazine about Ellis Island. Some influential people interested in preserving Ellis Island for posterity started a campaign to secure funds for the preservation of this historic edifice.

A couple of years ago, Lee Iacocca volunteered to head up the organization to preserve Ellis Island. His parents were immigrants from Italy who came through Ellis Island, as did so many thousands of others.

An appropriate monument - called the Wall of Honor - was designed and built on the island. Names of immigrants were inscribed on it so that future generations might know some history of the melting pot of this great county of ours.

Since my parents came through Ellis Island, I felt obligated to have their names inscribed on the Wall of Honor. I felt sure that documentation would be required. I wrote my sisters and brother to see if they had any knowledge of our family.

I was referred to a nephew, who I had never met, for information about our family. He was the grandson of my father's sister. He knew very little about the family history, but he did furnish me with a photo (about 75 years old) which happened to be a picture of my dad, his brother and his two sisters. I never knew the picture existed, but I did remember meeting these folks on a trip to New Jersey when I was about 6 years old.

I received a couple of letters from this nephew and one of the letters gave me a good chuckle. He had heard that I'd gotten married while in the service in Texas during WWII to a beautiful young lady who was kin to the infamous Jesse James.

Well, it so happens that I did marry a Marie James, whose father's name was Jesse James; but he wasn't kin to the infamous character. I'm sure that disappointed my nephew since he appeared to be sincere about the whole affair.

I'm sure there were some tall tales told about me since I did not return to Pennsylvania after the war - except for occasional visits.

I was in Germany during the war and did occupation duty for several months afterwards. At one time we were located in a village near the city of Passau on the Danube River in the Bavarian Alps. The Hungarian armies disbanded in this area immediately after the war and many families followed the army until the end of the war.

Since we were required to wear our Army helmet liners with our last names imprinted on it, I was frequently stopped by Hungarians in the area. The name Szalay is a typical Hungarian name, although it was not as popular as Jones in the States.

I hadn't spoken much Hungarian after the age of 17, since I was not with the family much after that time. However, I was familiar enough with the language to get by and carry on a conversation with the local folks.

One day we took the local brewmaster to Passau to buy some yeast on the black market so he could make beer for the occupation troops in our village. We let him make the rounds all day, since it took that long to make the proper connections.

While he was doing his thing, we walked around the city to take in the sights. At a shoe repair shop we inquired about having some boots made. While waiting, I overhead two shoemakers talking in Hungarian. They were among those driven from their homes during the war.

I heard one of them say "I wonder where these soldiers are from?" I introduced myself in Hungarian and they were amazed at my flawless command of the language. I told them my parents were born in Hungary and gave them the name of the village and county.

One gentlemen knew the village and promised he would look up the Szalay family there. Of course, he didn't know when he would have an opportunity to go there because of travel restrictions.

Some years later, while visiting my Aunt Mary in Duquesne, PA she said she received a letter from her hometown about the Szalay family. The writer said he had met me and had promised to send a message to my kin in my parent's village. What a beautiful surprise. A celebration was held with toast of wine and pilenka (whiskey).

Oh yes, dad finally got to visit his homeland after her retired from the steel mill. He spent three months visiting the folks in his village and was hailed as a returning hero from the land of opportunity.

And, yes, my parent's names will be inscribed on the Wall of Honor in 1992, when a second wall will be erected on Ellis Island.

Some Characters Last Forever
Sunday, January 19, 1992

I was born a few years after the turn of the century and raised in Duquesne, PA.

Duquesne is about 10 miles south of Pittsburgh along the Monongahela River in the foothills of the Allegheny Mountains. It is also in the midst of the industrialized steel mill area.

Duquesne was a melting pot of almost every nationality on the European continent, as were most of the towns up and down the river.

The influx of all the immigrants during this period caused numerous communication problems since very few could speak a word of English. Many of these people had skills they brought with them. Those skills helped them get employment in spite of the language barrier. There was also a need for unskilled laborers in the many factories, steel mills and coal mines in the area.

With the collapse of communism in the Soviet Union, we are again hearing names like Serbia, Yugoslavia, Croatia and others that were dormant for many years during the rule of the hammer and sickle. All the nationalities were part of the melting pot that settled in these industrialized areas.

The newcomers brought their skills and their customs of the old country with them. Among the customs was a practice known as mid-wifing. A midwife is a person skilled in assisting the birth of a child.

Back in Duquesne, she was usually middle-aged or older and had the experience of giving birth to several children and assisting in delivery of any number of children. Normally a midwife had very little formal education in the art of child delivery but the people who needed her service couldn't care less.

A good midwife was also an excellent cook who would perform these and other household chores for several days. She would also assist with the care of the newborn until the mother was physically able to assume the responsibility of running the household.

My father worked in the steel mills as did many of his friends and acquaintances. The men worked 10-12 hours a day in the scorching heat of the open hearth furnaces where the steel was being made. The men had to wear special dark glasses and heat resistant clothing while working around the hot metal.

After a hard day's work, the men would usually stop at the nearest saloon and gulp down a double whisky with beer for a chaser to clear their throats and lungs of the steel dust and other pollutants.

The personnel department of the local steel mill had a man on staff who could speak several languages. He was foreign-born, probably of Slavic ancestry and could speak some Polish, Hungarian, Russian and Czech. His services were most essential since the hiring of people who couldn't speak English would have been most difficult.

Because of his favored position he made many friends with the immigrants. And although it was never proven, he probably had a sizable income from under-the-table dealings in securing employment for his many friends and acquaintances.

There were other town characters, most of whom were well liked.

We didn't have an official town idiot, as was the custom during the days of the Roman Empire, but we had others. On payday we looked forward to waiting for the town drunk who would buy ice cream cones for all the children in the immediate neighborhood.

The most popular character was a gentleman known by the entire community as Chicago Mike. He would walk the streets picking up cigarette butts along the curb and go merrily on his way. He was well-liked and never got into trouble. The only thing he wouldn't do was work. In spite of this fault he was able to get free meals from people in various neighborhoods including ours.

I remember my Aunt Mary feeding him on several occasions. He would sit on the back porch and she would bring him whatever leftovers we had. He always needed a shave, but his clothes never seemed to be excessively soiled.

I remember he had the bluest eyes that I've ever seen. He never would say much, but he would always say thanks after the meal before leaving.

Chicago Mike lived on a bluff a short distance from town. From his perch overlooking the town of McKeesport, across the river, he could see all the hustle and bustle of the town business district. No one knew exactly why he preferred this lifestyle because he seemed to be a fairly intelligent person.

His living quarters were under a large slab of rock which partially sheltered him from the elements. In the winter, the heat from the burning mines nearby would keep him from freezing.

Some of the old-timers who knew Chicago Mike said he had been living this lifestyle since WWI. It was believed that he served overseas during the war. It was told that he wrote letters to his lady friend who lived in McKeesport. He planned to marry her when he returned from overseas after the war was over. When he came home he learned that his lady friend had already married.

Chicago Mike was so heartbroken that he made a vow to never work again. He would just sit on the bluff and gaze at the bustling crowds across the river. His lady friend lived in the area and he could stare at the crowds hoping that maybe she might think of him.

Years later Chicago Mike died at his favorite home on the bluff. The severe winter was more than his ailing body could withstand. The townspeople mourned the death of their favorite character. He was given a pauper's funeral.

The steel mills also died the past few years. Foreign competition sounded the death knell. It affected the towns of Duquesne, McKeesport, Homestead, Braddock and others along the Monongahela River.

This is a sad day for the people of the area. This is a sad day for our country. This is a page of history that we shall regret and surely will haunt us for years to come.

LESSONS LEARNED DURING DEPRESSION
Sunday, March 1, 1992

Those of us who lived through the Great Depression like to tell our children and grandchildren about our experiences. The stock market crash occurred in the fall of 1929. It didn't have an immediate affect on most of the working class, but it did have a devastating affect a short time later.

People who invested in the stock market felt it immediately. The value of stocks plunged dramatically. Many banks went bankrupt and depositors lost their life savings. The president of our local bank committed suicide.

I remember people climbing coal cars of trains coming through town and using clubs to dislodge huge amounts of coal so it could be picked up by family members who walked along the tracks with buckets to retrieve it.

Since we had coal-fired furnaces, this method of getting the winter's supply of coal was very inadequate. Several families decided to open up their own coal mines to get their winter supply of fuel. Western Pennsylvania was coal mine country so we didn't have to go far.

The first task was to find a location to open a mine. One of the members of our family group had experience in coal mining. He could tell by the rock and soil formation on the side of the mountain where a seam of coal was likely to be. My dad and the other men went to work clearing the soil and rock for the mine opening. The seam of coal was found after a minimum amount of digging.

The toughest job I had in this operation was hauling a load of burlap sacks to the job site. I had a little red wagon loaded down with about 100 sacks that I had to carry from town.

The mines were called bootleg coal mines since the owners of the land did not know that these operations were going on. All we knew was that some wealthy individual in California owned the land. The land wasn't fit for anything else since poison ivy and scrub growth was all that could survive. The coal was of poor grade.

Since money was scarce, a deal was struck with a local truck owner. We would pay him in coal for each load he delivered. This way he got his winters coal supply and made expenses by selling what he didn't need. We got our coal supply with a very minimum of actual cash expense.

At the beginning of the depression, the steel mills were still operating. In the process of manufacturing iron and steel, there is a waste byproduct called slag. Slag consists of impurities containing sand, pig-iron and other residue. Usually slag is hauled off in a molten state in specially designed ladles mounted on railroad cars. The molten slag, which resembles hot lava that spews out of volcanoes, was dumped into hollows some distance from the steel mills. It took several days for this slag to cool and form a permanent fill.

It takes American ingenuity to realize that this cooled slag actually had some value. There was a certain amount of pig-iron that could be salvaged from it. Work had slowed down in the steel mills and the paychecks were rapidly dwindling. Men had time on their hands, so out came the sledgehammers. Usually other family members joined in. It was hard work and the pay was not much, but a family could make a few extra bucks to buy groceries. The pig-iron sold for a few cents a pound, so people flocked to the slag sites.

Entertainment was something that you just dreamed about. If it cost money you did without. Children were always resourceful, especially when they had no money. We found out that street car passes were sold each weekend for 30 cents. They were good from midnight Saturday to midnight Sunday. About noon on Sunday we would go to the streetcar stop area where passengers would be getting off from work or other trips. We would ask them if they needed their passes anymore and many would oblige us. We would take the next streetcar and ride all over the county for the next few hours. Many times we would go to the museum and library in Pittsburgh and spend the afternoon taking in the sights. Forbes Field was nearby and we would take in a ball game from the windows if the Pirates were playing that day. We would usually get back home at a reasonable hour after a very eventful day.

An enterprising neighbor showed me a fabulous offer he found in a magazine. He wanted me to become a partner. I agreed and he sent off the application to sell small vials of perfume for 10 cents a vial. I don't remember the number of vials we had to sell, but it must have been several hundred. After the appropriate number of units were sold, we would be eligible to receive a model airplane that we could actually fly.

After much anticipation the package finally arrived. We immediately started selling the perfume door to door in our neighborhood. Sales were hard to come by and after weeks of door knocking we had sold only a fraction of our inventory. We finally decided to send what money we had and the remainder of our stock back to the promoters. This was done only after numerous threatening letters from the promoters were received.

We were disappointed because we had big plans to learn to fly that airplane. To an 11 year-old kid, such an experience ended a very real dream that could not be forgotten for a long time.

Many lessons were learned during the depression years. We learned to be frugal and to appreciate all the wonderful things that life has to offer. It's unfortunate that our present generation has missed out on these lessons that we learned during the Great Depression years.

OLD COUNTRY REMEDIES CAN HELP
Sunday, March 22, 1992

Life in the 30s was far from routine for the folks who lived in western Pennsylvania. The bitter winters and the "Great Depression" took its toll. Record snows also added the challenges of survival.

I remember when I was in the first grade, dad had to help us walk to school in the deep snow. It was all uphill with no road to lead us to our destination.

Of course this was the short cut that we were using and it was only one-half mile or so compared to the two-mile route by road. Dad wore a pair of homemade metal gaffs to dig into the snow to keep from sliding on the treacherous slopes. The stories of the old timers walking to school uphill both ways, barefooted in deep snow was not all fiction.

I remember one winter when the Monongahela River froze solid from bank to bank. According to the old settlers this had never before happened. The river traffic was halted for several days. Hundreds of boats pushing 10 to 16 barges loaded with coal down the river daily to the power plants came to a halt. Finally in desperation one enterprising boat owner determined to get through the ice decided to use his paddle wheel to cut a path in the ice. This was not the book solution, but it did help to get traffic flowing in a few days. These river boat captains were a salty breed and they helped to keep the lights burning by getting coal to the power plants.

As we grew older we managed to make the trip to school during the winter a welcome experience. We learned to skate on the sidewalks without the benefit of ice skates. After a few falls, a few scratched arms and legs we managed to become proficient enough to get to school without serious injury. Of course this was all downhill. We never could come up with the solution to skate uphill.

I think our generation invented skiing. We didn't have any of the modern day equipment, but we did like they did in the Old Country. We improvised.

Old curtain rods were ideal for skiing downhill. Of course, borrowing these from the household reserve could be hazardous to your health. Barrel staves from old potato barrels were another substitute; however, you could not obtain the proper speed from these skis unless you were coming down Cemetery Hill. Cemetery Hill was also a sled rider's paradise. It was quite hazardous since it made an abrupt curve near the bottom of the hill. If you managed to clear this obstacle, you could consider yourself a pro. If you didn't you could consider yourself badly bruised or slightly immobile.

Some of the more mischievous types found other ways to entertain themselves during these bitter winter snows. These were the older teenagers.

I remember one time when they borrowed some metal gliders and chairs from a local clubhouse to use for their downhill skiing enjoment. They had a real fun time that night, but they paid the price when their identity was disclosed to the club officials soon after their night of fun and games.

I rarely had the opportunity to go to a movie but somehow I managed to accumulate the necessary funds (10 cents) to see "The Trans Atlantic Tunnel." It was in the fall of the year with a brisk wind blowing about 20 miles an hour when I arrived at the local theater. The movie was very interesting and I really enjoyed it.

As I left the movie, I suddenly realized that a blizzard was in full force. I couldn't even see across the street. The temperature had dropped into the 20s and visibility was down to zero. It was a three-mile walk home and I was not prepared for this brutal weather.

My ears begin to get extremely cold and I would cup my bare hands over my ears to try to warm them. I would get out of the wind by stopping at the store fronts while I was in the business area. When I finally got into the open area, I started to run as fast as I could. I finally got home with frozen hands and frostbitten ears.

Folks from the Old Country always had remedies for all kinds of ailments. My Aunt Mary was no different.

Realizing what pain I was in, she immediately escorted me down to the basement. This was the coldest part of the house and it was the best place to be with the problems I had. In a few minutes, she had the first aid remedy for my frostbitten ears. One large cabbage leaf on each ear wrapped in cheesecloth around my head.

I spent a miserable night, but by morning the pain had somewhat subsided. My ears were enlarged about three times their normal size; but by the third day when the cabbage leaves were removed, they were back to normal. Once you are frostbitten you can no longer stand the cold like you used to. You learn that in a hurry. I have never forgotten that lesson.

Back in the 30s we had snow storms frequently. Snow would be standing most of the winter. One of my chores was to shovel the snow from the doorway to the street. It seems like this was a never-ending chore every winter.

Many times I would be out shoveling snow after dark and again first thing in the morning. I didn't mind it so much at night since there was a certain beauty with the moonlight bouncing off the fresh fallen snow. Usually it was brutally cold and I would be thoroughly chilled by the time I would finish my task.

We had a remedy for this ailment also. Homemade grape wine. My dad made a 50-gallon barrel of wine each year.

This was made the Old Country way. The grapes would be tromped with bare feet. Family friends would be invited to help with this chore. Apparently this gave it the proper flavor that everyone enjoyed.

I would partake of a glass of this fine wine to thaw out after an evening of snow shoveling. I'll assure you that you could shovel snow in your underwear after a glass of this Old Country remedy. They don't make wine like that anymore.

DURING THE 20S, WE GOT AROUND
Sunday, May 10, 1992

One of the most important events I remember from childhood is the historic cross-Atlantic flight in the "Spirit of St. Louis."

Col. Charles Lindbergh landed in Paris after making a solo flight from New York to Paris in 33-1/2 hours. The year was 1927. I remember whistles sounding off from hundreds of Pennsylvania steel mills. Church bells rang out throughout the entire town. What a great day it was. History in the making and we were part of it.

Newspapers were about the only communication that reached the masses. If some very unusual event occurred, an "Extra" was published and was usually hawked by paperboys at daybreak. In order to qualify as a paperboy for the "Extra" one had to have a powerful voice that would wake up the folks. Extras were published in times of disaster - such as floods, major fires, election results, train wrecks and other unusual events.

Radios were about the only other method of communication to reach the masses. However, only the more prosperous could afford such a luxury. We had a thoughtful neighbor who enjoyed listening to the Pittsburgh Pirates baseball games and he wanted to share his enjoyment with his neighbors. He opened the front window of his home, placed the radio close by, turning it up full volume so all the folks in the neighborhood could hear. That's sharing! The neighbor, Mr. Weber, had a flourishing plumbing business.

Another one of our more prosperous citizens, named Shoulder, had a son who owned a two-seater airplane. He flew out of Bettis Field airport, about five miles from our town. I'm sure most of his trips were business, but some were definitely for pleasure only. On each return, he would buzz his homeplace to let his mother know he was coming home. The whole town knew when our illustrious pilot was returning from a trip.

The only public transportation we had were street cars and trains. However, there was no local transportation. To get somewhere locally, we walked. The trains and street cars were for transportation to towns up and down the Monongahela River.

The nearest big city was Pittsburgh. Many of the immigrants who settled in the area never left town. I remember dad riding a bicycle to work. Usually he walked to work in the steel mills, but for a few months he was assigned to a more distant part of the mill that required other mode of travel.

Automobiles were owned by the more affluent. We usually knew most of them by name since they were not that plentiful. Five families - out of 100 - that went to our church had automobiles.

I remember the first car I owned. It was a 1928 Whippet coupe with a rumble seat. My cousin acquired this relic from a friend so he could use it as a trade-in. It seems that the dealer would give a premium for a trade-in to induce you to buy a new car. Of course, he would increase the price of the car you were buying in order to make the profit he desired. Then the dealer would give the old junker back to you as a goodwill gesture. That's how I got my first car.

The dealer delivered it to our driveway in the alley. I told him I couldn't drive, but that if he would give me a few minutes instructions I could handle it. Using the dashboard, which was laden with a thick coat of dust, he drew in the gear locations and told me to use the clutch each time I changed gears. In a few minutes he was on his way and I took complete charge.

After starting the car a few times, I got bold enough to slip it into gear. The car lunged forward a few feet and I immediately jammed the brakes to stop. After a few more dry runs I slipped it into reverse. This happened to be a mistake since it lunged backward several feet before I could stop it and rammed into the neighbor's fence. The neighbor didn't know about it for several days and when he found the damage he decided to repair it without questioning aloud how it happened.

After several more attempts, I finally got the car out of the alley to the main road. I managed to drive it a few blocks to a large open field, where I had plenty of room to maneuver and get the feel of shifting gears without fear of running into any obstacles. A few days later, I secured a driver's permit and eventually got my driver's license.

I loved the old Whippet even though it made a weird whistling sound that could be heard a block or so away. Some of my friends wanted to know how fast my old relic would go. We decided to go to the most modern highway around, located near the edge of town, for a speed test. It was wide enough for two cars in our lane so we started out with our friend's car parallel to mine.

I started out slowly and gradually picked up speed. I finally let the hammer down and I knew I was going the fabled "60" with the whistling noise growing louder. I hollered over to my friend and told him I was at maximum speed and he said, "You are going 45 miles per hour." Nevertheless, it was a real thrill and the disappointment wore off without any ill affects.

But our primary mode of transportation was walking. I never did consider it to be unusual to walk anywhere. We walked to school, church, grocery store, ballgames and other places we needed to go. I remember walking to the Pretzel Factory in McKeesport. It was about a five mile hike by shortcut.

I had heard about the bargains at the Pretzel Factory. For 10 cents, one could get a basket full of broken pretzels. I managed to accumulate the necessary funds and took off at daybreak to get there at the magic hour. After arriving, a young lady came to the door and told me they didn't have any broken pretzels that day. The man who breaks pretzels was off that day. I learned at an early age that life has its disappointments.

My dad had a craving for cool spring water during the summer months. A mountain spring was located in the Union Woods, some five miles distant. At the appointed time, I would get two one-gallon jugs and take off for the famous spring. I usually enjoyed the walk since most of it was in a rural area.

Usually the trip was routine and uneventful - except one time. It was late one summer afternoon with the sun sinking low. I got to the spring without incident and filled up my jugs and started home. All of a sudden it turned cloudy and started to rain.

Soon lightning filled the sky and thunder roared with a deafening sound. I started to run, but the weight of the jugs slowed me down. I had to stop several times to catch my breath and the rain kept coming down and the lightning kept bouncing all around me. I was totally drenched and my shoes were filled with water.

The lightning was fierce and darkness was upon me. For some reason, I wasn't frightened. I guess I didn't realize how hazardous it was walking in such a storm.

Eventually I got home and was greeted by my dad. He was almost hysterical but was relieved that I made it home okay. I haven't been back to visit the spring in the Union Woods and I'm sure it no longer exists.

But surely in this great land of ours there still exists "Union Woods Springs," to quench the thirst and comfort the weary traveler.

OLD WORLD REMEDIES SEEMED TO HELP
Sunday, August 2, 1992

Before the advent of modern medicine, childhood diseases were the order of the day.

The early settlers brought with them remedies that had been used for generations in their homeland. Almost without exception, eight or more children in a family would be the norm of the times. Contagious disease would strike one of the children and then it would spread through the entire family.

Most cities had ordinances to help control the spread of diseases by posting "Contagious Disease" signs on the homes of infected persons. The city health officer would see that the rules were enforced.

No person infected was allowed to leave the posted premises. After the prescribed period of time, the health officer would fumigate the house to help keep the disease from spreading in the community.

On rare occasions, a doctor would make a housecall and prescribe some medication. Since most of these families were poor, they would use their own Old World remedies.

Most of the diseases - like scarlet fever, measles, diphtheria and others - would go through a cycle of about 30 days. Staying in bed, drinking plenty of liquids and eating homemade soup would be the best remedy. The natural defenses of the body would eventually take over.

Whooping cough was a common ailment that almost every child would get. It would usually spread throughout the family in a few days. The most common remedy was the use of goose grease.

The goose grease would be heated enough to feel warm when it was rubbed onto the chest area. Then a heated layer of cheese-cloth would be placed over the area. A heavy comforter would be used to cover up the patient. This procedure would be used each night for several nights until the patient got well.

There was one problem that had to be considered. Where do you get the goose grease? You either had to have a friend who had a supply of goose grease or you had to run down a goose.

The common cold also had an Old Country remedy. For children, hot tea with an ounce of homemade wine at bedtime was a sure cure. Store-bought wine would not work, so you had to make arrangements to get homemade wine.

We always had a good supply since dad made a 50-gallon barrel each year. The secret of making good wine was using the proper type grapes and using the same charred barrel each time.

It was customary to have two or three friends involved in the wine-making event. These friends would help in the grape-tromping custom which was brought from the Old Country.

Tasting of the wine would take place every few weeks during the fermenting process. A family get-together would be held on these occasions with plenty of food and last year's wine.

Adult common colds were treated differently than children's. You would use hot tea, but you added homemade hooch. During prohibition, there was no legal whiskey available, so you had to buy moonshine from a friend. My dad would send me to Polish Hill to a widow lady's home to get our hooch.

Everyone knew she made moonshine, but the law didn't bother her. She had a large family and had no other source of income. I remember she had five daughters who were quite attractive, but they were much older than me. The price of this homemade remedy was $1 per quart.

The cure for minor stomach ailments was a homemade remedy that reminds me of Alka-Seltzer. You would mix about an ounce of vinegar, about four ounces of water and a teaspoon of baking soda. Then you stir like crazy and drink it as fast as you can. This was a refreshing drink and it did cure most minor stomach ailments.

For the more serious stomach problems, you would drink a tall glass of chilled sauerkraut juice. Of course, it had to be homemade to get the maximum benefit. Fresh cabbage was used in making sauerkraut and the fermenting process had to take place in a crock container. No other container would do since the acid of the juice would otherwise change the final result. This could be detrimental to our health.

There was one sure cure for most health problems. Chicken soup.

Homemade chicken soup was one of the most-used medications for many ailments. The custom was known throughout Europe. Every patient recovering from an operation would be spoon-fed chicken soup. This custom is still followed in many hospitals in Europe today.

Almost every country in Europe had bands of gypsies roaming the countryside. They lived outdoors most of the time and lived off the land. Their good health could be attributed to eating wild berries, grapes, apples and other wild fruit and game made into a stew. Of course, using a chicken or two from some local farm would add flavor to the stew.

Many gypsies migrated to America during the turn of the century. They brought their customs with them and they still like to roam.

Indian tent shows were an annual attraction in the 20s. They always sold health remedies made from herbs and other wild growth. Their famous elixir was made with about 20 percent alcohol. It was the greatest medication available to make you feel great.

During the Great Depression, the typical family fare of our house was homemade soup. For 25 cents you could buy an adequate amount of soup meat and bone to add flavor to your soup. For a few more cents you could buy enough vegetables to satisfy the average family.

Of course, parsley was an herb that was essential to giving the soup the exciting flavor that all great cooks used. Mother's homemade noodles made this soup a real treat. We were getting our vitamins long before it was the popular thing.

Although there is no scientific evidence to prove the value of most of the cures mentioned here, the old-timers still believed in them. If it helped them, that was all that mattered. There were no side effects to worry about.

HARD TIMES MAY BE THE BEST TIMES OF ALL
Sunday, December 13, 1992

The Christmas season in Hungary began on December 4. This was St. Nicholas Day and it was time to put your shoes outside the door for St. Nicholas to bring gifts of fruit and nuts. That is if you were good, but if you were bad your shoes would be filled with ashes. This was the custom in all the villages on the plains of Zemplain where my parents were born.

The Christmas tree was picked out months in advance and was brought in from the fertile fields a few days before Christmas. Ornaments and other decorations were scarce so dried figs and other dried fruit was hung on the tree.

Several days before Christmas baking of kalaches would begin. There were raised dough loaves filled with ground English walnuts, creamed cottage cheese, sweetened poppy seed, raisin and prune preserves. There were also huge loaves of bread made from the sweetened raised dough.

Fresh pork and smoked pork was usually the main dish and everyone looked forward to enjoying these special holiday foods for several days.

Gifts were something that were reserved for the wealthy who lived in the larger towns and metropolitan areas.

Everyone attended church services on Christmas Eve and all joined in on the carol signing. Christmas was a very joyous occasion and the celebration lasted several days. After church services the children would go carol singing in the village. They would call on all the homes of parishioners and sing two or three songs at each house. There were adults who accompanied them and they would accept money for various church needs. The caroling would continue on Christmas Day and after until all the parishioners were called on. The children were offered goodies at each house and that was their gift for caroling.

These same customs were brought to Duquesne, PA and continued for several years. I remember walking through the snow the night before Christmas going caroling until about midnight. We would begin again the afternoon of Christmas Day and make rounds of parishioner's homes for several hours. It would take about three or four days to complete our mission of visiting the homes of all church members.

At our house we had a small artificial tree that was decorated with ornaments that my parents bought shortly after they were married. I still remember the dried figs that were hung on the tree. We also had a few candles that were hung on the tree that would be lit when company would arrive. We would stand around the tree and sing a couple of Christmas carols. Then we would blow out the candles so that they would be available for our next guests arrival.

Since the depression years occurred about the time I was growing up, my parents were not able to buy us gifts. I had four sisters and a brother and living in a steel mill town was not the place to be during these lean years. Since dad worked in the steel mills two or three days a month, it was not near enough to provide the very essentials of life. Our parent's life savings were used up to see us through these difficult times. Insurance policies were cashed out to pay the interest on the mortgage.

During these years at Christmas time, boxes of Christmas candy were given out at our local public library. The mayor of our town, Mayor Crawford, made arrangements with the local steel mill, with the aid of his brother who was general manager of the steel mill to donate this candy. It was a generous size box of hard candy, about a pound, that was decorated with Christmas wrapping. This was the only gift that hundreds of families would get for Christmas. We had to stand in line for two or three hours, usually in the snow to get this gift. I remember doing this for three or four years during the Christmas holidays. I'm sure the custom has stopped since the need no longer exists. Just recently I heard that the beautiful old library was torn down. It was built before the turn of the century and donated to the city by Andrew Carnegie, the multi-millionaire philanthropist.

During the holidays, the more affluent kids in the neighborhood would share their gifts with us. The new football was put into play a day or two after Christmas. There were enough children around to pick out teams of touch football most anytime. After the ground thawed out, we would play tackle football in a vacant lot.

The new bicycles and roller skates would have to wait for warmer weather. The little red wagons would come out regardless of the snow and bad weather. The sleds were shared as soon as snow arrived. We had plenty of hills for sled riding. We would stay out in the snow for hours riding sleds until our feet and hands were so cold that we could hardly move. This is what was called fun!

After the holidays, all the kids in the neighborhood would round up Christmas trees. We would build a huge bonfire in a vacant lot and stand around and watch it burn. We couldn't afford marshmallows, but we managed to get enough potatoes for everyone. If you haven't eaten roasted potatoes with about one-half inch charcoal around it you have missed a real treat.

WORK ETHIC DIFFERENT DURING 30S
Sunday, February 7, 1993

During the 20s and 30s in order to survive in the industrialized areas of Pittsburgh-Duquesne, PA children would go to work at an early age.

The father was the breadwinner of the family and the mother had a full-time job taking care of the children. The population consisted of numerous ethnic families who had come from the old country to the land of milk and honey.

Because they couldn't speak English, these immigrants had to accept low-paying, unskilled labor jobs. The children went to work after school and during the summer to supplement the family income.

It was unusual for the foreign-born to be considered for any job other than common labor because of the language barrier. If your parents were born in America or migrated from England, your opportunities were considerably greater.

"Johnnie Bulls" (anyone who spoke English or of English ancestry) were the elite of the society and got the best jobs. Since our parents spoke very little English, we didn't have many opportunities to learn the language.

When we started school, our teachers were burdened with the various ethnic children who spoke very little English. However, children learn quickly at that age and it didn't take long to grasp the new words and become familiar enough with the language to get along.

Our parents didn't have many opportunities to learn English. We always lived in areas with people similar backgrounds, so ethnic languages were always spoken. Shopping was always done in stores where ethnic languages were spoken. Most stores had personnel who could speak two or three languages.

Our parent's education consisted of schooling of three or four months during the winter for two or three winters. Everyone six years-old or older worked in the fields on the vast fertile plains of Hungary.

The Great Depression brought on by the stock market crash of 1929 made earning a living more difficult. The steel mills were the primary source of employment for most of the laboring class.

The steel mill in my hometown, Duquesne, employed approximately 5,000 men. In the early 20s, a seven-day-a-week work schedule was the norm. This continued until the Depression, at which time the work week consisted of five days and gradually dropped to one day a week.

In view of the hard times, it was imperative that the children find some kind of employment to add to the family income to help meet the bare essentials of survival. Since I was the oldest boy of the family, it fell on my shoulders to help in some small way to bring home the bacon.

The first job I remember was working in a butcher shop delivering groceries in my little red wagon. I was only 10 years old, but I was required to do many chores in the market.

Cleaning the meat block every evening at closing time was the toughest job. My work schedule was from 7:00 a.m. to 8:30

a.m. and 4:00 p.m. to 7:00 p.m. each weekday and 7:00 a.m. to 11:00 p.m. on Saturday. For all these hours, I was paid $2.50 a week.

Another job I remember is working for the local fruit vendor by the name of Sam Sofer. Sam would go to Pittsburgh to the produce market each morning in the summer at about 4:30 a.m. I would meet him at the outskirts of town at about 7:30 a.m.

Of course, I had to walk about five miles to the meeting place. Then I would be given two baskets of fruit or vegetables (whatever was in season) and go door-to-door selling the produce. Mr. Sofer would move his truck slowly down the street as I made the rounds. He would always remain close by so I could get refills when needed.

One summer I went to work on a chicken farm for Fred Wohleen. The farm was located near Murrysville, which was about 25 miles from home. I had several chores to do each day.

This farm was on US Highway 22, a well-traveled highway even back in the early 30s. My bedroom was located downstairs facing the highway. The trucks rolled all night long.

Mr. Wohleen had a Gulf service station that was open part-time. If someone wanted gas, the driver would blow the horn and I would come a-running to take care of his needs. The station was located next to the house, but I usually would be some distance away in one of the chicken houses.

I was about 13 when I worked at the chicken farm. It was my job to gather eggs each morning after breakfast and bring them to the house. There were about 2,000 laying hens and that kept me busy for most of the morning.

Another hired hand about 16 years old also worked at the chicken farm. He hauled the feed into the chicken houses and did some of the other heavier chores. He also milked the cow each morning and evening.

After I had been working about two weeks, the hired hand told me he was going to go on vacation a couple of weeks and I would have to milk the cow while he was gone. Mr. Wohleen couldn't milk or do very much because he had serious back problems.

I watched the hired hand milk the day before he left and he gave me some instructions. The next morning I was up by daylight and I went to the barn to do the milking.

I got the bucket in place and got the stool positioned properly and started to milk.

Old Bessie slapped me on the face a few times with her tail, but I kept milking. The flies were bothering Old Bessie, so she started to kick with her hind legs. Somehow she managed to get one foot in my milk pail when I was about half through milking.

I managed to get her foot out of the pail and finished milking. I had to skim the dirt off the top of the milk so Mr. Wohleen wouldn't see the mess I made.

I was pretty proud of myself for the first-time milking experience. I improved a little each day.

I also solved the tail-slapping problem by tying her tail to her leg while I was milking. Old Bessie didn't like it very much, but we managed to get along for the couple of weeks that I had to milk her.

Yes, these were the good old days. It was a great experience and it's nice to sit back and reminisce.

OLD COUNTRY FOOD IS SPECIAL
Sunday, May 9, 1993

Most everyone has memories of his heritage that were handed down by parents or grandparents. My parents were born in Austria-Hungary and immigrated to America about the turn of the century. I never had the opportunity to meet my grandparents.

My parents and many of their friends lived in the same town in the foothills of the Allegheny Mountains and brought many of the customs of the old country with them. The town of Duquesne, PA, 10 miles south of Pittsburgh, was no different than other large industrialized towns in the area. Numerous ethnic groups settled there and worked in various factories and steel mills.

Every ethnic group had its favorite holidays and annual picnics and outdoor dances to celebrate the occasion. Beauty contests were held, speeches were made and other activities were provided for various age groups. Favorite ethnic foods were served and all enjoyed themselves. Draft beer seemed to be a favorite drink at all these ethnic gatherings. Music was always furnished by their own talented husbands and sons who were familiar with the old country songs. Occasionally gypsy musicians who migrated from the old country were hired to provide the music.

The one custom I remember was the greeting of strangers. If they spoke your ethnic language they were immediately your friends. Then eventually you would visit them and be treated like long lost kin. Their best homemade wine would be brought up from the cellar and good food and fellowship would be the order for the day. Many of the friendships lasted for years.

One of the family friends I remember was a John Kiska. He was about my dad's age but short of stature at five foot two. He was a comical gentlemen and a good storyteller. Before he would start his storytelling, he would get his pipe ready for the occasion. It was not the standard smelly pipe.

This special pipe looked like a miniature saxophone about three foot long. It would hold about a third of a can of Prince Albert. At the end of the pipe stem was a tobacco container that had a lid on it that controlled the amount of air being fed into the pipe. By adjusting the lid you could make the tobacco burn slow or fast. Because of the length of the pipe stem, the smoke would be cool by the time it got to your tongue.

The stories that I remember Mr. Kiska telling always had a humorous ending. They would almost always take place in a small village. The main character would usually be a stranger who would come to the village on the way to some other more distant place. He would spend the day usually getting into mischief and by day's end would be run out of town. These stories were usually intended to entertain the children, but usually the parents would take part and enjoy the stories as much as the children.

The story-telling custom came from the homeland. During the long winter nights some of the friends would get together and visit just to pass the time. There would always be someone who would take over as the storyteller. Usually the men, would take turns and the children would sit in front of the stove or fireplace and enjoy the stories. The ladies would do their crocheting and exchange the latest gossip of the village.

I remember some of the most beautiful crocheting that I had ever seen was done by my mother. Many hours were spent on just one item. My favorite was a fancy fruit bowl design. When all the crocheting was completed the finished product was soaked in a starch solution and placed over an appropriate size fruit bowl.

It would be pressed against the bowl and left to dry into the exact shape of the bowl. About 24 hours later, when the starch solution was totally dry, the bowl was removed and you would have the most beautiful crocheted fruit bowl you have ever seen.

There are certain ethnic food items I used to look forward to eating at certain times of the year. Hog killing time was one of my favorites.

Living in the city, we didn't kill hogs but our local butcher did. Other country style bacon (fatback), that was trimmed about three-fourths inch thick and seasoned with a heavy coating of paprika, was one of my favorites. Of course, regular slab bacon properly trimmed and seasoned could be substituted if desired. In order to enjoy this delicacy to the fullest, you would invite some of your friends over for the occasion. First of all you built a fire large enough to accommodate all your friends. All of this took place in the privacy of your own yard. Green switches of adequate length or some homemade metal skewers would be used to hold the bacon. The bacon would be cut about two-thirds of the way through and placed on the switches. A medium-sized onion was then placed on the end of the switch. You held the bacon over the fire and turned it slowly until the bacon drippings started to flow. You would have your rye bread ready to catch the drippings and would continue until all the drippings ceased flowing. Then you would cut the bacon and onions and place them on the rye bread, add some hot or mild mustard and your sandwich was ready to eat.

The children and ladies would be served milk or their favorite soda and the older men would usually have a snort or two of their favorite hooch. Remember, this was the time before cholesterol was invented.

Another delicacy I enjoyed was Hungarian-Style pigs feet. This is a seasonal item and should be made only after the first cold spell when the temperature drops to the 30s. Have your butcher slice the pigs feet lengthwise and also cut into about three pieces per half. Use about one pint of water per pigs feet. Season with several buttons of garlic and add enough paprika to color your stock a mild red. Simmer for several hours or until pigs feet separate into several pieces. Let cool and place in soup bowls and refrigerate until the stock has jelled. Eat cold as a main dish with rye toast.

Sun-cured pickles is another recipe brought from the old country. Use about a dozen medium sized cucumbers quartered about two-thirds of its length. Place in a crock container and cover with boiling water. Sprinkle liberally with dill and other pickling spices. Slice two loaves of rye bread and place in a crock. Place weight over all the above to submerge all ingredients and set outside in the sun. Temperatures should be in the 90s or above and the curing should required three to five days. Yeast in the bread hastens the curing process. Remove pickles from the brine when thoroughly cured and refrigerate. Eat with your favorite meat dishes.

Many of the ethnic customs may be forgotten unless we take immediate steps to preserve this heritage. Fortunately, there are enough interested ethnic groups in various parts of this great country of ours who are doing something to preserve these beautiful customs.

MIXTURE FORMED NEIGHBORHOOD
Sunday, July 4, 1993

Politics where I was born and raised near Pittsburgh, PA was typical of politics in other industrialized areas of the east.

Politicians in towns like my hometown of Duquesne usually stayed in office for several terms. Mayor Crawford was re-elected numerous times and served 20 years. The local vote was controlled by a handful of businessman and the top executives of the local steel mills. Since there was only one major employer (steel mills) in town, you voted according to their wishes if you wanted to continue working.

There were many ethnic nationalities living in my hometown and most of them worked in the steel mills. We had a mini United Nations that consisted of Serbs, Czechs, Poles, Hungarians, Slovaks, Hebrews and several other ethnic groups living in town.

It was not uncommon for over-the-fence squabbles between the various nationalities because of some mischievous behavior of their children or some other insignificant incident in the neighborhood. This was a century-old problem that we can see happening in Europe today. Unfortunately hundreds of people are being murdered and thousands more are left homeless and starving because of ethnic problems.

In order to maintain order among these ethnic groups, our city fathers hired members of these groups to serve as police officers. If trouble arose, police officers could be dispatched who spoke the language and problems could be resolved before things got out of control. Most ethnic people living in this area could speak little English, so it was essential that proper personnel could be sent to the troubled area.

When election time was approaching, Mayor Crawford would round up 50 to 100 children from the poorest neighborhoods and buy them each a pair of new shoes. This was certainly a great thing to do before election time to remind people how well off they were with the present political administration. Politics today are no different. The strategy is the same but the approach may be different.

The school system was not immune to the political control by the city fathers. There were two teachers, a brother and sister, of ethnic origin who were hired by the school board. Normally these jobs lasted a lifetime. However, it didn't apply to ethnic teachers. After only a year, both of these teachers were replaced with Anglo instructors. There was no charge of incompetence or any other problem that the school board would admit to. There were no priorities established for ethnic teachers.

I was a senior in high school when this happened and all the students were up in arms about the dismissal of these two teachers. Some of the leaders of the student body decided that we would go on strike in order to show our school board that we wouldn't accept their decision.

Word was passed around during the weekend and all students were advised to join the strike and march around the perimeter of the high school Monday morning. There was almost 100 percent participation Monday, but some of the students started back to school the next day.

By the end of the week only about a fourth of the students were still on strike. No one was disciplined for participating in the strike. The school board got the message and that was the last time they tried anything like that.

Politics and management of the steel mill administration held a steel grip over the employees. This lasted a long time, but eventually the employees got their fill. The union became active and people started to join and get involved.

The union was gaining strength and as time passed it got stronger. Within a five-year period, the union got strong enough to have a candidate for mayor. Mr. Maloy ran for mayor and beat long-time Mayor Crawford. The entire political machine didn't fall apart suddenly, but it did weaken as the new political system took over. An informed electorate can also change things in our time.

Our chief of police was an Irish man by the name of Flynn. He was a likable person who was chief for many years. He never did anything outstanding, but he did small favors for people regardless of their ethnic background or status in the community.

He would ride around in his squad car, up and down the various sections of town, to let people know he was available. It was not unusual for him to pick up someone who, after a snootful of whiskey, was having a hard time finding his way home. The chief would never prefer charges against these characters because he felt that they were not troublemakers. All they needed was some help to get home.

There was an unusual character on the local police force by the name of Sullivan. He operated the hand-controlled traffic light in downtown Duquesne. This was the busiest traffic intersection in town. There was a major railroad crossing, street car crossing and other traffic in the area.

I remember seeing him operate the traffic controls when I was about 14 years old. He was chubby, with a pot belly like Santa Claus. He had rosy cheeks and his lips seemed unusually red. I found out later that he used makeup and that's why he had rosy cheeks and red lips.

Nothing unusual happened in our hometown except the school strike. Duquesne was a typically quiet steel mill town located along the Monongahela River.

However, something happened that made the headlines in all the newspapers in several states. Constable Gallagher, a brother to Matt Gallagher, the town's popular druggist, got orders to pick up Sullivan, the policeman who operated the traffic light. Constable Gallagher didn't have any details and didn't know why he had to take Sullivan to City Hall.

On the way to City Hall, Sullivan asked Gallagher if he would stop in at the nearby saloon for a drink. Gallagher felt there would be no harm in having a drink with his friend Sullivan. They entered the salon and had their drink.

While there, Sullivan asked to use the restroom and Gallagher gave him permission. After several minutes Gallagher went to check on his friend and found the restroom empty. Sullivan crawled out of the restroom window. Gallagher left immediately to see if he could find his friend. He was nowhere in sight. Gallagher called City Hall and gave the report of the missing Sullivan.

Tragedy struck several minutes later. Sullivan made the rounds of his accusers and killed eight people. He had been molesting a little girl and his well-kept secret was a secret no more. Sullivan apparently knew that the word got out about his behavior, but Gallagher was not aware of these serious offenses.

Sullivan was eventually convicted and given the death sentence.

History repeats itself and we must learn to live with these terrible events until we can find some solutions that will put an end to such tragedies.

DEPRESSION LESSONS LAST A LIFETIME
Sunday, August 22, 1993

Many lessons were learned during the Great Depression of the 30s. The stock market crash in the Fall of 1929 affected the lives of everyone. In the steel mill city of Duquesne, PA the two banks were on the verge of bankruptcy. The steel mill owned the majority of stock in the banks and saved the banks from closing their doors. Lifetime investments became worthless overnight. One lesson was surely learned by everyone who was old enough to know what was happening. Frugality! Ask anyone who lived through those Depression days and they will tell you what hard times taught them.

I was next to the oldest of six children and being the oldest boy, it became my lot to help with the family income. I was 10 years old when I started to work for our family grocer. I worked after school and all day Saturday for $2.50 a week. The Saturday schedule was from 7:00 a.m. until 11:00 p.m. The child labor law didn't apply during the Depression, if it did it was totally ignored.

Most of the family grocery shopping was done on Saturday because of the lack of refrigeration. A block of ice was purchased Saturday morning from your local door to door iceman to preserve the meat and other perishables for weekend consumption. You placed the colored card in the window on Saturday morning. One side of the card had a figure 25 and the other side had a figure of 50. This helped to speed up delivery since your friendly iceman knew what size block of ice you needed.

I remember one very good customer we had at the grocery where I worked. The family consisted of the mother, father, two daughters and a son. The two daughters weighed about 250 pounds each and the young son, about 12 years old, weighed about 200 pounds. On Saturday they would buy a whole pork loin (equal to about 15 pounds of pork chops), 50 pounds of flour, 50 pounds of potatoes, one 25-pound sack of beans and numerous other items. The Meisters were one of our best customers. The two girls worked for Westinghouse and apparently had some Depression-proof work.

Another good customer was the Teischarts. Mr. Teischart was some sort of an official in some local business and was making a good salary. They bought steaks almost everyday. They had a charge account at the store as did most of the customers. They had two boys who did most of their shopping. They boys were about 16-18 years old and they both smoked cigarettes. Since they didn't have a job, they didn't have money to buy cigarettes. They would have the owner, Mr. Schwartz, charge the account with 40 cents worth of steak to pay for their cigarettes. As far as I know, the boys were never caught making this false entry in their grocery accounts.

I held several other jobs while attending school. When I was 15 years old, I worked at the Allegheny County Fair which was held a week before Labor Day. The fair was located at South Park which was about 15 miles from home. It was also about 15 miles to Pittsburgh. I got a job selling Zig-Zag (now known as Cracker Jack). The pay was based on commission. I would checkout a carton containing 100 boxes which sold for 5 cents a box or a total sale price of $5 per carton. The commission was 50 cents per carton. The best salesman would get a bonus of $1 each day. I got the bonus a couple of times until some of the kids pooled their sale and beat me out of my bonus. I walked through the grandstand which seated 100,000 people selling the Zig-Zag from about 11:00 a.m. to 10:00 P.m. We had a favorite spiel we used while hawking our Zig-Zag. "Its good for the ladies, won't hurt the babies and gives the old man an appetite."

I had to walk home the 15 miles since I couldn't afford to spend my earnings on bus fare. Occasionally, I would get a ride for a short distance but most of the time I had to walk the entire distance. The trip took about four hours and I can assure you that I was totally beat by the time I got home.

I had a neighbor who had begged me to take him along to work at the fair. Steve was a little younger than I but had the desire to work. On the way to work we could take shortcuts across fields and old country roads to save a couple of miles. After walking in the grandstands all day long in the heat, we were both pretty well beat. We started for home at 10:00 p.m. and when we got to the nearest village (Broughton) about 10:30 p.m. Steve was too tired to go any further. We found a small country rooming house that had a vacancy so we stayed there for the night. The room cost 50 cents for the night so we split the bill. It felt good to get a good nights sleep after making the 15 mile trip for four days. The next morning we had breakfast which cost us 25 cents each and was on our merry way to work the last day of the fair. My total earnings for the seven days was $16.

On our way home the last day, Steve told me that their milkman lived near the village of Broughton. He delivered milk to the Duquesne area so we decided to locate him and spend the night. After making a few inquiries, we found our way to the milkman's house and arrived about 11:00 p.m. the milkman's wife told us that her husband left at 1:00 a.m. We didn't get much sleep before we were awakened to get ready to leave at 1:00 a.m. We helped with the door to door delivery and finally got home about 6:00 a.m. What a way to end the summer vacation and start the first day of school.

I wouldn't want to live through these "good old days" again but I'm glad I survived these hard times. I learned many lessons which lasted a lifetime. This experience prepared me for the military service that Uncle Sam thought I needed in WWII. It also helped me in my life's work and also prepared me for my retirement years which I am certainly enjoying.

ELLIS ISLAND VISIT RECALLS FAMILY ROOTS
Sunday, October 24, 1993

Ellis Island is a symbol of America's immigrant heritage. For more than six decades, 1892 to 1954, the immigrant depot processed the greatest tide of humanity in the nation's history.

Some 12 million people landed there. They came from almost every civilized nation in the world. The greatest number came from Europe. Today their descendants account for almost 40 percent of the country's population.

Ellis Island ushered in a new era of immigration with each immigrant's eligibility to land to be determined by federal law. The federal government established a special bureau to process the record numbers that were arriving daily.

Hundreds of steamships were built to accommodate these masses of humanity. Steamship owners were making fabulous profits, unheard of prior to this immigration explosion. First and second class passengers were processed on board ship, but third or steerage class passengers were ferried to Ellis Island where they under-went medical and legal examinations in the Main Building.

The first and second class passengers were the more affluent type that the steamship lines catered to since their fare was considerably higher than the third class passengers. In addition, these passengers spent money on the other luxury items that were available on most all of these steamships.

Medical personnel boarded the ships to examine the first and second class passengers in the harbor where the ships dropped anchor. These medical exams were mostly visual and it was almost a foregone conclusion that all would pass. The steamship owners and medical personnel were on friendly terms and probably worked out some financial rewards for the medical personnel.

The third or steerage class passengers were ferried to Ellis Island where they underwent medical and legal examinations in the Main Building. These were thorough examinations and all the immigrants feared the outcome. Most any kind of rash or skin irritation would disqualify these passengers. This meant a return trip back to the port of origination. The steamship lines were responsible for returning these immigrants without any cost to the passengers.

Fortunately only two percent of all the immigrants entering this country were disqualified for various reasons. What a terribly traumatic experience to be saddled with. Families would be separated and the fear of never seeing each other again was frightening.

The trip from most ports in Europe took at least 30 days. Storms in the Atlantic could cause additional delays of five to 15 more days. The steerage class passengers would be called on to help pump water from the ship's hold during storms.

What prompted these masses to risk everything to come to this land of opportunity? Freedom!

The entire continent of Europe was almost constantly in turmoil. From the turn of the century on, people feared war was inevitable. They wanted to leave for fear of their lives. They fled from hardships such as poverty, religious persecution, or political unrest in their homelands.

During the peak periods of immigration, Ellis Island would process as many as 5,000 people a day. They would be checked, questioned and sent on their way. The processing took between three and five hours. For others, a longer stay meant additional testing. And for an unfortunate two percent, it was exclusion and a return trip home.

Ellis Island bulged at its seams. Originally a 2-1/2 acre island, barely visible above high tide, the land expanded over the years to 27-1/2 acres. A total of 35 buildings were added to accommodate the needs of the immigrants during the peak years.

Despite the growth, the island facilities remained inadequate (except during the immigration lull of WWI) until 1924. After that, quotas on immigration drastically stemmed the tide.

On Nov. 29, 1959, the government closed the island and it remained abandoned until President Lyndon B. Johnson placed the deserted facility under the care of the National Park Service on May 11, 1965.

Very few funds were available for the upkeep of the buildings on Ellis Island. The buildings began to deteriorate and were left in a state of disrepair. Finally, in recognition of the significant role Ellis Island played in American history, the Main Building was refurbished in time for the immigration depot's centennial in 1992.

Centerpiece of the restoration project was the construction of the Ellis Island Immigration Museum. The museum tells the poignant story of the immigrants who entered America through the golden door of Ellis Island.

About two years ago, I happened upon an article in a magazine regarding a project to be constructed on Ellis Island to honor all immigrants who came to America since 1892. Lee Iacocca, former president of Chrysler Corporation, was the prime mover of this project. Since his parents, who were born in Italy and went through Ellis Island, Iacocca felt a deep obligation to honor them and all other immigrants with an appropriate edifice to be constructed on Ellis Island.

Since my parents came to America through Ellis Island, I immediately felt a deep desire to get involved. I wrote to the Ellis Island Foundation to get all the facts so I could take necessary action to participate in this project.

I was informed that a "Wall of Honor" was being built and names of immigrants would be inscribed on a stainless steel plate that would be mounted on a concrete wall outside of the Main Building on Ellis Island. A $100 fee would be assessed for each name to defray some of the expense of the construction.

I wanted my brother and three sisters to become a part of this project since it should become a family project. After numerous phone calls and letter writing we got all the data together to proceed. Our family is scattered over several states which caused some of the delay.

After much research we still didn't have all the facts we needed to establish proof of our parent's entry into this land of freedom. We did finally get the date of entry of my father and mother from the naturalization office in Pittsburgh, PA. My father arrived May 1909 and my mother arrived May 1915.

Through correspondence with the Ellis Island Immigration office, we learned that proof was not required to have our parent's names inscribed on the "Wall of Honor." We immediately sent our money in and received an appropriate certificate officially certifying that our parent's names would be inscribed. The certificate was signed by Lee Iacocca.

The first phase of construction of the Wall was being completed at this time, so we were placed on the second phase of construction. The second phase was to begin in early 1992 and it would require several months to complete.

We had planned a family reunion to visit Ellis Island and view the "Wall of Honor" as soon as the second phase was complete. Several weeks ago we received word it was complete and our parent's names were appropriately inscribed.

The date was set for the family gathering for Sept. 17, 1993. In Rockville, MD with the trip to Ellis Island on September 20. My daughter made the trip with me so we could get the younger generation involved in the history of our family. We hired a limousine service to take all the family from Rockville to the ferry in New York Harbor.

The ferry ride took about 25 minutes. It made a stop at the Statue of Liberty, which is only a few hundred yards from Ellis Island. Since we had only about four hours to spend, we passed up the opportunity to visit the Statue of Liberty.

Upon entering the great hall of the Main Building at Ellis Island. I saw hundreds of people who seemed to be deeply engrossed in the viewing the photos of the immigrants. I felt a certain warmth that I never felt before.

I was walking in the very footsteps of my parents who came through these very portals years ago. I could feel the anxiety my parents surely endured as they waited for their final approval to enter this land of freedom. Then I searched out their names on the "Wall of Honor," located just outside the Main Building.

I had to touch the place where their names were inscribed. All this was a very moving experience that would surely touch the souls of all who would come to visit Ellis Island to honor their parents.

AUTUMN IS AN ARTIST'S DREAM
Sunday, November 28, 1993

Every season brings with it its own beauty and wonders that last for a lifetime. Autumn was always one of my favorite seasons of the year.

In the foothills of the Allegheny Mountains where I was born, the fall color was an artist's dream. Just a few miles from the steel mills of Duquesne, PA the hills were covered with trees that had leaves of every shade of red, yellow, orange and brown.

A drive into the rural areas along country roads was always a treat. The squirrels and rabbits would be hustling up and down the ravines gathering acorns, hickory nuts and other wild growth for their winter supply. Occasionally a deer would dart across the road and be out of sight in an instant.

Once in a while we would stop and admire some late blooming wild flowers. We even dug up some of these to plant in our flower garden. We later found out that wild flowers do best growing in the wild where nature intended them to be.

Once in a while near a fence row we would find a quince tree that was easy to reach. Quince is a yellow colored fruit about the size of an apple that is used to make jelly or jams. It is a very bitter tasting fruit, until after a frost which causes it to mellow and sweeten. We learned in a hurry that biting into a quince before it has mellowed would sure cause you to pucker in a hurry.

Sometimes along the fence rows we would find apple or pear trees with a late fall crop that we would have to sample. Usually we would gather up enough of these to take home to have pies or jelly. It could be hazardous to your health to climb the fences to retrieve some of the fruit if some farmer happened to have his shotgun handy.

Wild grapes seemed to be plentiful at some locations. They would usually grow along rows of trees and would spread for several hundred feet. I was never hungry enough to taste these grapes for I feared that they would be unfit for human consumption.

Crab apples were plentiful in some areas and were usually bitter to the taste. The first frost would cause these apples to mellow and sweeten somewhat. We never cared much for this fruit but many folks made jelly from this wild apple.

If Gypsies happened to be in the area, they would make some sort of a stew out of the crab apples and other wild growth. Gypsies lived off the land and seemed to be a healthy race of people. It was not uncommon for them to make a midnight requisition for a hog or some chicken near a farmhouse, adding flavor to their gypsy stew.

The fall of the year was also a time to gather vegetables from the garden and put them up for the winter. We would usually have carrots, turnips, cabbage, kohlrabi and onions that we would store in the ground to be used during the winter months. A trench would be dug about two feet deep. A layer of vegetable would be placed at the bottom of the trench. Then a layer of sand would be used to cover the vegetables.

This method would be used with each layer being covered with sand. The top layer would usually be about the level of the adjacent ground. Then a dog shed-type building would be placed over the top layer to protect the vegetables from the elements. A door would be installed at the front of the shed large enough to reach in to retrieve the vegetables. We never lost any vegetables due to the most severe winters.

During the depression years of the 30s, many people had victory gardens. These gardens were located a short distance beyond the city limits where land was available. The gardens were intended for those folks who had no garden space at their houses.

Plots of ground about 50 feet square were allotted to each person who was interested in having a victory garden. The plots were marked off and numbered so they could be readily found by their owners. A caretaker was on duty to oversee the entire project.

The government furnished the seed at no cost and all one had to do to qualify was to sign up and abide by the few simple rules. The land was also free so it was a good deal for anyone who wanted to have a garden and enjoy the fresh vegetables during the growing season. Many people took advantage of this opportunity and enjoyed the fruits of their labor.

Another important event in the fall was the annual corn and wiener roast sponsored by the local volunteer fire department. Almost every volunteer fire department in western Pennsylvania got involved in this type of activity as a money-making project.

The roasting ears were placed in huge drums of boiling water and were steamed until tender. Several handfuls of husks were cooked with the roasting ears to enhance the flavor. They gave off an aroma that would draw the crowds to buy this gourmet treat.

The wieners were cooked on homemade grills that were fired with wood salvaged by local volunteers. This was one treat we looked forward to each year even though the weather sometimes was not conducive to this outdoor activity.

Yes, autumn is one of the most beautiful times of the year that we should look forward to and enjoy to the fullest.

DEPRESSION TEACHES LESSONS
Sunday, January 16, 1994

The one thing that the Great Depression of the 30s taught us was to improvise.

If you lived in the steel mill area anywhere from Pittsburgh, PA down the Monongahela River for 15 miles, you were forced to learn this lesson in order to survive. The steel mills in Homestead Munhall, Braddock, Duquesne, McKeesport and other towns along the river were operating at about 10 percent capacity most of the time.

Growing up during these times was a daily challenge to children as well as adults. Being one of six children, I always had plenty of chores to do. Household chores were something we all had to get used to doing.

The steel dust from the local mills caused me a lot of grief since I had to sweep off the two large porches almost daily. Usually every Saturday I had to scrub the porches to get all the buildup of steel dust that the sweeping didn't accomplish.

We did manage to find some time to enjoy playing with the neighbors after the chores were done. There were plenty of children in the neighborhood so it was never a problem to get enough kids together to play games.

The alley behind out house was our recreation area. We played mush ball, using a homemade bat. If someone got a real bat for Christmas, we would use it. A mush ball was similar in size to a real softball, but it was also homemade. Once in a while we would have a real softball if someone got one for a birthday gift.

We had to learn to hit the ball within the limits of the alley. Otherwise it would be an automatic out. Some of the neighbors didn't like to have our mush ball coming into their yards. They would keep the ball if we didn't get if before they had an opportunity to retrieve it. We would remember these people on Hallow-een and would hang their porch furniture on the nearest light pole.

Another favorite game was playing cowboys and Indians. We made guns out of pieces of apple boxes we got from the local fruit peddler. We would shoot rubber bands that were made from old inner tubes.

Everyone had a different design for his homemade rifle and the idea was to have a long bore so the rubber band would be stretched to its limits. The longer the bore, the more distance you could get when you released the rubber band. If you were close enough, you would get a pretty good sting if fired at your britches.

The homemade scooter was another invention of which we were proud. We would mount an old pair of roller skates on a two-by-four about three feet long. We would use two wheels in front and two wheels in back and an upright made of a two-by-four with a handle to hold on to. It was great fun riding down the sidewalks with this homemade marvel.

Hoops were another item that we made by using a potato barrel stave nailed to an old broom handle. This gadget would be used to guide a wheel that we started in motion, then chased up and down the sidewalks of the neighborhood.

Doing this daily for about an hour would keep us in shape. We wouldn't have the energy to get into any mischief after these workouts.

Miniature golf was another outdoor activity we invented. We made our golf clubs out of fruit and vegetable boxes that our friendly neighborhood grocer would give us.

We would usually have one or two yards in the neighborhood that were level enough to use for our golf course. A two or three hole course was as large as we needed. Miniature golf courses were soon being built by local entrepreneurs who made a good living from our ideas.

Playing the game of marbles was another favorite pastime. Almost everyone received marbles for Christmas or birthdays. For a nickel we could usually buy a sack of marbles that contained about 25 multi-colored beauties.

The space between the curb and the sidewalk was the favorite place to play this game. A circle about one foot in diameter was described in the area that was to be used to place about 20 marbles.

A line, used as a starting point, was marked about 10 feet from the circle. The shooters would line up. A marble would be placed between the thumb and index finger. Then the shooter would release the marble with the maximum amount of force in order to hit the ring of marbles and to dislodge them from the ring.

All the marbles knocked out of the ring would belong to the shooter. The next shooter would get his turn when the present shooter would miss getting a marble out of the ring. A good player could eventually win all the marbles.

Baseball cards were a popular item and every kid managed to accumulate a few. We would get a baseball card with every purchase of a one-cent stick of gum. The gum and card were about four inches square.

The baseball card had a picture of the player on one side and a brief summary of his career on the other. My favorite team was the Pittsburgh Pirates and I traded my cards for my favorites. Occasionally I would keep cards of other teams if they were the well-known players like Dizzy Dean.

We learned many lessons during the Great Depression years. Learning to improvise was certainly one of the most useful and beneficial lessons.

During my teenage years and later, as I matured, I used my boyhood experiences many times. It served me well and I am thankful that I had the opportunity to live through these memorable years.

Our present generation of teenagers would do well to have had such experiences.

JUNIOR HIGH YEARS WERE BEST
Sunday, February 20, 1994

My favorite school years were at junior high school in Duquesne, PA. I remember well when I was 12 years old and a seventh grader.

I started school when I was 5 years old and went to school with my older sister, who started the same year as I. Early school enrollment was not encouraged but was authorized if classrooms were available.

Discipline was strict and we were expected to behave like mature adults. When the bell rang to change classes we were expected to immediately proceed to our next classroom.

Loud talking or loitering was not tolerated. After the final class of the day, at 4:10 p.m., we marched out of school keeping in step with the piano music played by one of the students.

Our teachers were great motivators during our junior high years. Everyone was encouraged to get involved in some school activity. Since I weighed about 70 pounds, I was not a good candidate for football or other similar outdoor sports.

My English teacher suggested that writing poems for our monthly school newsletter might be interesting. After some deliberation I finally decided to join the poetry club.

At our first meeting we were given some instructions and rules to follow and then we were on our own. I was a total blank until I started to stare out the school window. I could see the hills were emblazoned with fall foliage and I soon had some subject ideas.

Within an hour I had written a four-stanza poem about the fall colors and the coming of winter snows. It was published in the next school newsletter.

I also became involved in school plays, although I did not volunteer for this activity; I had no choice. I played the part of Brutus in the skit, *"Julius Caesar - A Tragedy by Shakespeare."* The skit had very little resemblance to the original play but I had fun doing it. After I killed Caesar, I had to haul him off stage in a wheelbarrow.

In the eighth grade we had a class in government and current events. Mr. Robinson was one of my favorite teachers. He could make the lessons so interesting that you couldn't help but learn the subject. He taught us how our government works and how bills were passed. The test was dull, but Mr. Robinson made it interesting.

We always spent a few minutes each day on current events. If the subject was newsworthy, we would devote more time for discussion.

The Lindbergh baby kidnapping happened during this time. Newspapers were full of stories about it, together with pictures of the Lindbergh house and the ladder (used in the kidnapping) leaning against the house. We were all saddened when Charles Lindbergh's child was found dead several days later.

Our English class in the ninth grade was also one of my favorites. We had to write themes consisting of 75 to 100 words. This was a daily assignment for most of the school term.

It was fun because the themes were usually based on some humorous event that occurred in the life of the writer. We had a lad named Chester who wrote some humorous stories. He was a slow-talking character who took twice as long to read his theme than anyone else in the class.

One day he was unusually slow, but his theme was very humorous. After the recitation, I glanced over to his desk and noticed that his paper was totally blank. He read the entire 100-word theme from an empty piece of paper. What an accomplishment!

We had another character who was one of the most popular kids in junior high. Everyone called him Shorty. He went out for football each year in junior high although he was mostly a bench warmer. He was about four feet six inches tall and weighed about 70 pounds in full football gear.

Shorty was loyal and never missed a practice. In order to qualify for a football jacket, you had to play at least four quarters. The coach would always put him in for one play each game. That one play would qualify as a quarter. Shorty managed to get a football jacket each year.

Our football stadium was about two miles from the school. Classes were dismissed at 2:30 p.m. on days when the game was being played at home. Season tickets were 25 cents, but only the more affluent kids could afford them. These were hard times and 25 cents was hard to come by.

I worked at a grocery store after school and didn't have time to go to football games, even if I could afford a season ticket. Kate Schiedler, owner of the store, let me off once during football season since business was slow that day. I walked out to the football stadium in time for the game.

I planned to view the game from Depression Hill, which overlooked the stadium. I met some of my buddies near there. They knew how to get inside without going through the gates.

There was a drainage ditch with a three foot culvert that entered the stadium behind the bleachers. We crawled through about 50 feet of culvert and were just in time for the beginning of the game. No one was guarding the area so we just stepped into the bleachers and took our place with the other students.

We whooped and hollered and had a great time. The band was seated at one end of the field where they remained during half-time. They played the school fight song and that was about all the half-time entertainment.

We didn't have all the pageantry we have today at football games and we didn't have chorus girls, high-steppers or flag bearers. We *did* have an abundance of enthusiasm and school spirit that money can't buy. And we enjoyed life to the fullest.

AIR CLEARED OF IRON ORE DUST
Sunday, April 24, 1994

Growing up in the steel mill town of Duquesne, PA you got accustomed to seeing every day clouds of iron ore dust in the air. You breathed it, smelled it and learned to live with it.

Pollution was a word that was not yet invented. The environmentalist would have had a field day with those conditions.

The trains carrying coal roared through town several times a day. The tracks were adjacent to the main drag of the town. Street cars also sped along the main street to add to the noise. Passenger trains also came through daily to add to the excitement.

The main gate to the steel mill was located at the junction of the two main streets which caused automobile and pedestrian traffic to be snarled during certain times of the day. Some brave soul would hop on the trains in order to get across the tracks if they were running late for their work shift. This could be hazardous to your health, especially if the trains were traveling at a rapid rate of speed. Some didn't make it.

The railroad had a man on duty at the crossing who would lower the gates several seconds before the train arrived. He would ring a loud bell to caution all the traffic before the gate was lowered. Of course many people ignored this warning and made a mad dash to beat the train.

The railroad man on duty was located in an 8x8 enclosure about 30 feet above the tracks so he could observe the oncoming trains in time to lower the gates. I thought he had the best job in town and I wished some day to have that job.

The street we lived on was not paved, but it did have crushed rock of sorts which served the purpose since there wasn't much traffic. In the late 20s the city began a street building program that included the street in front of our house.

I spent some of my spare time, when I wasn't doing chores, watching the men work. It was hard labor since very little machinery was in use at that time.

A cement base was mixed and poured as the foundation of the street. The bricks were laid by hand over the cement after it had cured for a few days. The bricks were about twice the size of bricks used to build homes today. Then a coating of hot tar was poured over the bricks to seal them from moisture. It seems like it took forever to finish our street, but I can assure you it was built to last and it did.

The dedicated postmen delivered the mail in the heat of summer and bitter cold and snow of winter. Our mailman would always read the postcards and would tell us when he delivered it that Aunt Suzie was having a big time vacationing in Atlantic City or whatever else was interesting in the card. Postcards were only a penny then and first class mail was three cents. Delivery was twice a day in some sections of town.

Small cars were not invented by Volkswagen. The first "Austin" was about the size of the "Beetle" and was first manufactured in the early 20s. It never did become popular and faded into obscurity after about a year or two.

There were other cars that were popular in the 20s - the Hupmobile, Whippet, Cord, Packard and Pierce Arrow, to name a few. Most of these went by the wayside.

I owned a 1928 model Whippet with a rumble seat and I had a lot of fun with it. I paid the total sum of $25 for it.

I never had a real store-bought haircut until I was a teenager. My dad cut my hair with barber tools he bought for about a dollar. The clippers were dull and I would lose part of my hair each time it was cut. The clippers would pull it out of my head.

On special holidays I would get a real haircut from a "bootleg" barber. It would cost about 10 cents. A bootleg barber is an amateur who had a professional set of clippers and whose shop was located in his basement and operated without a permit.

One of the first parachute jumps ever made was at Bettis Airport near my hometown. This event was highly publicized and people from miles around came to witness it. The jump was made from about 3,000 feet, out of a two-seater, open cockpit plane.

The jump occurred at night with floodlights illuminating the sky and following the plane and the parachutist as he made his jump. The charge of $1 per vehicle paid for this historic event. I was there.

The most important political event I can remember was when Franklin D. Roosevelt was campaigning for his first term as President of the United States. Every major street in town was lined with townsfolk. It was the first time that any person running for this high office ever visited our hometown.

OLD CUSTOMS TAKE ROOT IN AMERICA
Sunday, July 10, 1994

Many customs of the Old Country were brought to America by the thousands of immigrants who came to this land of freedom about the turn of the century.

My parents were no different. They settled in the steel mill country in Duquesne, PA. My dad always had a supply of homemade wine and beer to share with visitors, friends and acquaintances.

During prohibition, whiskey - more commonly called "moonshine" - was a little more difficult to purchase. Bootleggers were the people who managed to deliver the homemade moonshine to loyal friends and customers.

At times the law would clamp down on the bootleggers - round them up and fine them - to show the townsfolk that lawmen were on the job. During these difficult times, it was almost impossible to find someone from whom to purchase moonshine. People used this potent drink for medicinal purposes in addition to treats at social gatherings.

I remember a buxom, friendly madam who came to our house one time when Dad was totally out of the famous elixir. She visited awhile and then went into the bedroom to adjust her girdle. When she came out she handed dad a bottle of moon, for which she was immediately paid. She promptly made her exit.

I remember another colorful character who was known as "Moses the Ragman." He was about five feet six inches tall, broad shouldered, husky looking and wore a black derby. He had a heavy beard that extended several inches below his chin.

Moses made the rounds of our town and we could depend on him being available at least once a week. On his back he carried a huge burlap sack loaded with rags, pieces of copper or brass and other items he would buy from folks on his route.

All the kids in the neighborhood would find something to sell to Moses for a couple of pennies. We looked forward to his visits to our neighborhood so we could make a penny or two, which we would promptly spend at the neighborhood candy store.

Moses rented a large metal barn down the street from our house where he stored his loot until he had enough to hire a truck to haul it off to market. Moses lived to be an old man and he practiced his trade until he died. It was rumored that he left a small fortune to his next of kin. He was a bachelor and apparently had no close relatives.

There was an elderly lady who made the rounds about once a week begging for food and money. She always wore black clothes and carried a basket. She would go door to door in our neighborhood. Most people would invite her in.

My Aunt Mary would always feed her and listen to her tales of woe. She told Aunt Mary she lived in Homestead, which was a town about 10 miles away. She always managed to get streetcar fare from one of the neighbors. The food and money was used to feed her family of several children, according to her story.

Several weeks went by and there was no sign of the little old lady. It was rumored she died and left a small fortune to her family. It couldn't be verified since no one knew where she lived.

Another character I was fond of was Tony, the water department employee. He was a rosy-cheeked, robust man who must have weighted 250 pounds. Every Friday he came into the meat market where I worked after school and bought a couple pounds of round steak. Friday was payday and he treated his family.

Tony always chewed on a small black cigar. I asked him where he got his rosy cheeks and he said that he made "Dago Red Wine" and he always had his glass of wine with his evening meal.

Tony the shoemaker was another colorful character. He loved smoking cigars and always had one in his mouth while repairing shoes in his shop. He spoke broken English but managed to get along with his customers in spite of this language problem.

Tony loved to swim in the Monongahela River, about five miles from his shop. Almost every Sunday during the summer he could be found floating down the river that divided our hometown of Duquesne and McKeesport. His pot belly would keep him afloat without much effort.

My cousin John would go down to the river on Sunday afternoons in the summer and swim for an hour or so. He was a good swimmer and could swim under water for quite some distance. He would always be accompanied by his brother and some friends.

On Sunday while swimming underwater, he apparently got the cramps and couldn't come up for air. His brother, who was about 12 years old, thought he might have swam across the river to the other shore. After sometime, they realized that John had drowned.

The River Patrol was notified and dragging operations began. Grappling hooks were used to drag the bottom of the river for a couple of hours, but to no avail. It began to get dark and the operation was about to be called off. Then out of nowhere an elderly man appeared on the scene.

The man held a Rosary in his hand and placed it in the water while saying a prayer. The Rosary started floating for a few feet and finally stopped. He told the River Patrol that the body would be found at that spot.

The grappling hooks were lowered again and as predicted, the body was retrieved. The elderly man disappeared before anyone got his name.

This incident was reported in the McKeesport newspaper and is probably filed in the newspaper archives of the early 1930s.

PENNSYLVANIA TRIO HEADS WEST
Sunday, July 23, 1995

After recuperating a few days from our trip to the East Coast, we decided to head West. It was mid-July 1936 and we were planning to leave from Duquesne, PA as soon as our plans were finalized. I recruited a couple of my buddies who seemed very interested in exploring the country on our way to the Golden West Coast.

We gathered up some blankets and canned food to take care of the immediate necessities of our trip. We also carried a few tools to do any minor maintenance of my 1931 Chevrolet.

No formal route was planned so we could change our direction anytime we decided to do so. After driving west for awhile, one of my two buddies suggested we go to Kentucky. Andy had a brother in a Civilian Conservation Corps Camp, better known during those Depression years as a CCC Camp.

After a leisurely drive of two days, we arrived at the camp in the hills of Kentucky. We were treated like royalty and fed a fine meal that first evening. It was about 8:00 p.m. when we arrived, so the cooks had to be called back to prepare a meal for us.

The next evening we were invited to go sight seeing up the Daniel Boone Trail. We stopped at an old farm house and our friend from the camp got out and visited with the family, members of whom were playing their stringed instruments and singing.

After a short visit, our friend returned and we proceeded up the trail for a short distance. We stopped and our friend got out and walked into the woods. In a few minutes he came out with a Mason jar hidden under his shirt. We drove up the trail for awhile and stopped at a clearing.

Our friend suggested we get out of the car and sample the stuff he had in the jar. He took a long snort and swallowed like it was cool lemonade. The jar was passed around and everyone took a little sip.

I took a long snort and almost gagged. Blue smoke came out of my ears and nose and I saw stars. I'll never forget my initiation to the good old Kentucky moonshine.

The next day we started again on our trip westward. We stopped at a remote village to get some gas. Since it was an off-brand variety, we decided to buy only 50 cents worth. After the old hillbilly pumped in our 50 cents worth, he said, "Tweren't much in there. Tain't much more in there now," I'll remember that phrase as long as I live.

The next day we stopped in a small town in Tennessee where a circus had just set up. We decided we would inquire about working there for a few days. I got a job hauling buckets of water to the elephants.

After a few trips I told my boss that I was hungry. He took me up to their cafe and told the folks to feed me. After a hearty meal I decided to leave the buckets there for someone else to water the elephants. I took off, found my buddies and we left in a hurry.

A day or so later, we stopped at a farm in Missouri and asked the farmer if he needed any laborers. He said he could pay us only 25 cents a day to hoe his corn and he would also feed us three meals a day. We were glad to take the job because we knew the home-cooked meals would be worth working for. We slept in the car, but we were used to that so it was no problem for us.

About three days of this work and we were off to continue our journey. A couple of days later we were pulling into Kansas City. A gasoline war was going on all over town. Gas was selling for 9 cents a gallon.

One enterprising station operator had a large sign posted in front of his station. It read: "Get your gas here and get a free car wash if you buy $1 worth of gas." We took advantage of that, because we needed the gas and the car needed to be washed.

We eventually reached Omaha, NE. I remember seeing on the highway a sign that looked like a town marker, "Boys Town, population 110." We decided to stop and see what this "Boys Town" was.

Well, it was a home for boys. Father Flanigan was the town's founder back in the late 20s. A movie with Spencer Tracy and Mickey Rooney was made in the 30s. It was a great hit.

We stopped in Omaha and bought a newspaper to see if we could find any work through the help wanted ads. We made one inquiry, a salesman job. We weren't interested and couldn't qualify anyway.

Douglas Street was noted for its saloons and nightclubs. We visited some of the saloons and talked to the bartenders to see if they knew of any available work. There was no good news about work in the area, according to the bartenders and patrons. We enjoyed the 10 cent beers and free popcorn. After visiting several joints, we decided to leave town.

One of my buddies decided he'd had enough of this traveling and wanted to go home. He hopped a freight train and eventually got back to Pennsylvania. This was a hazardous way to travel and we were sure relieved when we got word he made it okay.

On the road again, we were headed for the famous corn country of Nebraska. We stopped at Neligh, NE, a beautiful rural city of about 1,000 people. We drove up and down Main Street and came upon the local pub. This was always a good place to get information.

The bartender promised to check with the local farmers who frequented his place to see if they needed any hands. There was a local depot where two trains a day stopped and picked up and dropped off mail and other freight items.

A boarding house near the depot housed the train crews and served home-cooked meals. The public was also served meals for 25 cents. We planned to stay in this town and enjoy some of that food.

We were hoping to get some good news within the next day or so from the friendly bartender. Well, no word was forthcoming, so off we rode into the sunset.

CALIFORNIA PLANS SIDETRACKED
Sunday, September 3, 1995

As we were leaving the beautiful city of Neligh, NE and heading west for California, we decided to make one more quick stop and say good-bye to our friendly bartender. Good thing we did, for he had good news for us.

The local county sheriff had left word that the county had two more vacancies to fill the quota for the Civilian Conservation Corps. We were told to go immediately to the county courthouse and to fill out the necessary paperwork.

There were two school teachers who worked at the CCC office who helped us fill out the various forms. They gave us permission to stay at the Girl Scout cabin that night. It was located a few blocks from the courthouse. We were to ship out the next day to our destination.

About 7:00 a.m. the next day, we heard a knock at the door. It was the two school teachers. They invited us to breakfast at the campgrounds. A hearty meal was prepared on the outdoor grill and they sat down and ate breakfast with us. They had our orders and we were to leave that morning for Columbus, NE.

There was one problem. We could not take our car to the camp. We didn't have much time to sell my 1931 Chevrolet, so we again approached our friendly bartender. After some discussion and several phone calls, the bartender said the sheriff was interested in buying the car. I sold it for $75.

That was a real bargain because the car was in good shape. We never had any problems all the time I owned it. Of course, I paid only $95 for it and I guess I got at least $20 worth of pleasure from it.

We arrived at our camp that evening and were assigned bunks in the barracks that accommodated all 60 members. There were separate quarters for the camp commander and his assistant. There were Reserve Army officers and the camp was set up like a typical Army installation.

We had a first sergeant, supply sergeant and several other non-commissioned officers with the rank of corporal and sergeant. the rest of us didn't have any rank and we were paid $30 a month. We received only $5 a month and the remaining $25 was sent home. We didn't have any formal drills or formations, but we did have a bugler who sounded off each morning at 6:00 a.m.

The Soil Conservation Service was in charge of our work schedule. They had offices on the grounds and the camp furnished them the employees to do drafting and other chores. They were in charge of the survey crew, also camp members who laid out the contours on the farms and did other soil conservation work.

We had a foreman and an assistant foreman who were in charge of the work crews. We would leave at 8:00 a.m. each morning, except Saturday and Sunday, in trucks to various farms that had signed agreements with the Soil Conservation Service.

In the summer we would gather up sacks of grass seed by stripping various blades of certain types of grasses that would be used to plant in washed-out and eroded farmland. We also built small earth dams where gullies were washing away top soil.

We always worked without shirts in order to get a good suntan. They were having a serious drought in the Midwest and the corn crop was a total failure for the past couple of years. The normal 50-60 bushels per acres was down to 10-15 bushels per acre.

There was a terrible infestation of grasshoppers. They would come in clouds that would devour a cornfield in a few minutes. We would hang our shirts on fence rows and the grasshoppers would eat everything except the collar and cuffs.

Watermelons were grown in some of the farm acreage that had sandy loam land. The watermelon crop was fairly good that summer, but the price didn't hardly pay to harvest the crop. They were selling for 5 cents each at roadside stands.

On day we were working near a watermelon patch on a hot day. We stole a few watermelons and had a feast. Since we had no knives to cut the melons, we dropped them on the ground so they would split. We would eat the heart out of the melons until we were stuffed. I got my fill and lost my appetite for melons for a long time.

In the winter we would install snow fences to keep the snow from blowing off the fields. In the spring the snow would melt and provide moisture for the arid soil. We would also dig holes in the frozen ground about three feet deep to prepare the soil for tree planting in the spring.

On weekends, there was very little to do unless you were on KP (kitchen police). I would be invited to go home with the Sullivan brothers on occasion. They lived in the small village of Hadar, about a three hour drive. I was there on Thanksgiving Day and looked forward to a big feast.

On Thanksgiving morning we went out into the woods to hunt for our dinner food. We killed a huge turkey and we had turkey and dressing for dinner.

On another weekend visit we went fishing. The little creek was frozen, so we had to do some spear fishing. We cut a hole in the ice and sent the neighborhood kids upstream to start tromping on the ice. As they approached our spear fishing point, the fish started to appear.

We speared about a tub full of fish and divided them among the kids who helped in the tromping. The Great Depression taught us all to improvise.

We had little money for entertainment since our $5 allowance was used for shaving supplies and other essentials. However, we managed to save a little of our allowance. Four or five of us would pool our money and buy a pony keg of beer (four gallons) and have a picnic with our girlfriends. We managed to get to town on weekends and meet local lassies.

We looked forward to these get-togethers since the long weekends were making most of us homesick. Well, we never did make it to California, but the experience we gained along the way made it all worthwhile.

TAKING A GAMBLE IN DUQUESNE
Sunday, February 19, 1995

My father took me to the first movie I ever attended. The year was 1925 and I was a mere six years old.

The theater was located in our hometown of Duquesne, PA. The film was the famous passion play that was heralded as the best of the silent films.

You had to read the caption on the bottom of the film to be able to keep up with the happenings in the movie. I couldn't read, but it really didn't matter. I'm not sure of the admission price, but 10 cents was typical price of the silent movie era.

It was about five years later when I attended the movies again. Well, I really didn't get to see this movie, which was a wild west film, because of some unanticipated developments.

The first feature was over at noon and we waited until everyone was leaving the theater. We slipped through the crowd and managed to get inside without being observed by the management. We got into the seats near the back row and waited for the next feature to start.

A few moments later, the manager turned on the lights and managed to see us trying to hide under the seats. He escorted us out of the theater and threatened us if we tried to sneak in again.

Sometime later, sound movies came of age. The admission price increased a few cents, but the crowds grew. The theater owners were doing quite well financially until the Great Depression hit in 1929. People were no longer able to afford the price of admission, which had increased to about 25 cents. In order to stay in business, theater owners had to come up with some gimmick. That's when Bank Nite was introduced.

It started out with a $100 prize each week. If there was no winner, the prize was increased to $200 the second week and would continue to increase $100 a week until there was a winner.

Each person would receive two tickets when he paid his admission and the stub would be placed in a large tumbler placed on the stage. The drawing would be held before the last feature. You had to be present to win and your ticket remained in the tumbler for each successive drawing. Many people deprived themselves of necessities in order to have the price of the movie on Bank Nite.

Years later, word got out that the winners of the Bank Nite were not legitimate winners. They were people the management had placed in the audience. Their names were called out as winners by some sleight of hand maneuver of ticket shuffling. I always wondered why the winners were always out-of-town folks who nobody seemed to know.

Things haven't changed very much down through the years. There is always someone out to make an easy buck. There have been all sort of scams around, years ago and still today.

Lottery is another popular pastime that has been around for years. When I was in high school, I had a part-time job as a numbers bookie. Each day a combination of three numbers taken from the total sales in the stock market would be the winning numbers.

The numbers kingpin was a neighbor of ours who seemed to be very likable. Most of the bookies were older men.

The numbers kingpin had an automobile repair business at this home as front to his numbers business. There were several bookies who worked for him full-time and they all appeared to be making a good living. Of course, the kingpin was doing quite well also. He always had a couple of new cars and wore fine clothes.

I was the only young bookie working for the kingpin and since I couldn't devote much time on the job, I didn't bring him much business. I made the rounds of my customers before school and used my lunch hour delivering my receipts to the kingpin.

My customers would only spend a nickel or dime on numbers so I really had to hustle to collect a dollar or so each day. My commission was 30 cents on the dollar and that was big money for a kid during the Depression.

I would usually spend a nickel or dime a day hoping to hit the numbers. I saved the rest to help buy some of life's necessities. I was living with my Aunt Mary and I tried to help with all the expenses of being a star boarder.

I sold dream books to my customers to make some extra money. This book interpreted all kinds of dreams with a series of three numbers. All my customers were great dreamers and they could hardly wait for me to arrive in the morning so they could play their favorite dream numbers. Those nickels and dimes spent on numbers made their lives more bearable during those days.

The postmaster's wife was a good customer. I would call on her Sunday night so she could play her variety number 410 each week. Her allowance must have been 10 cents a week for numbers because that is all she spent.

Another customer was an elderly couple. The husband had a favorite way of picking his numbers. He used a magnifying glass to find his numbers on a daily comic strip. Somehow he managed to find numbers on the comic strip characters.

I believe some people could find numbers in the air. I guess it took a lot of concentration to be able to find numbers in thin air and other unusual places.

Booking numbers was an interesting and sometimes hazardous business. The local police would have an all-out drive to apprehend bookies and the kingpin every few months. The ones caught would pay a fine and then business would return to normal in a few days. We usually got word in advance when the police raid was expected and we just had to be more careful.

After being in the business several months, I, like my customers, started to have dreams about numbers. I would spend as much as 25 cents on some of these dream numbers.

One morning, when I awoke I had a real gut feeling about playing number 701. I spent 30 cents on this number and low and behold at 5:00 p.m. that evening, the stock market number I played hit it right on the nose. I won $135.

I was the happiest person in the world. I felt filthy rich for the first time in my life. I bought a beautiful 1931 Chevrolet four-door, maroon sedan for $90 and lived high on the hog for several days.

Today, lotteries are great money makers for several of our states and are making new millionaires almost every week. Spending money on lotteries can become hazardous to your health, so don't let it happen to you.

Be very conservative and enjoy the fun and maybe someday you will become a millionaire.

SOMETIMES THERE ARE MIRACLES
Sunday, April 30, 1995

Life for a teenager in the 30s in Duquesne, PA was probably no different than in any other city in the country. I guess every young boy experimented with smoking corn silk wrapped in newspaper.

It only took a couple of puffs to realize that the taste from the burning newspaper tasted awful. The flavor from the corn silk wasn't all that bad. Usually one experience of smoking this stuff was all you needed to convince you to stop this foolishness.

My dad ordered tobacco from Mayfield, KY during the depression years. A 10 pound bundle of tobacco leaves cost a couple of dollars. Dad rigged up a cutting board to cut the tobacco into long grain bits fit for smoking in a pipe. He never did inhale but he enjoyed the strong flavor and aroma of this Kentucky burley.

I got bold and tried it once and I got woozy very quickly. That cured me of smoking for a long time.

One of my teenage buddies was a lad we called Sweet Sue. He liked to tinker with old cars and do maintenance on them. One day he got a bright idea to build a "race car" from an old junker.

He rebuilt the body and shaped it with a pointed front and back to look like a race car of the 30s. The starter on this car would not work so it had to be pushed off to start. I went with him to try out this new-fangled contraption and it was a thrill.

After driving around awhile, he decided to try a steep hill to see how the vehicle performed. Since the brakes weren't too good, he asked me to get down to the bottom of the hill to halt traffic so he could make the turn at the intersection of Crawford Street hill and the main thoroughfare.

I positioned myself at the intersection and halted traffic as the racer reached the bottom of the hill to make the turn. He spun around the turn on two wheels and eventually came to a screeching halt. I had my thrill for the day and we were lucky we didn't get caught by the local police for doing such a stupid thing.

There was a young Armenian teenager who was a local character. Sam was about 16 years old and was built like a brick wall. He must have weighed 200 pounds or more.

Sam worked as a hod carrier for various brick layers in town. It is one of the toughest jobs anyone can imagine. He spoke broken English and had a hard time getting any work at all because of the language problem. We used to tease him a lot and being good natured he never seemed to mind it one bit.

We taught him a song or two and would have him sing to us everytime we met him. He would roll those big brown eyes at us and sing like a bird.

Beer gardens were part of the scenery in almost every neighborhood in Duquesne. There was one I remember near the outskirts of town on Bull Run Road.

An elderly gentleman was the bartender and owner. He was a hulk of a man who kept order in his place of business. State law required that one meal a day had to be served to qualify for the beer license. Ethnic meals would usually be served in these neighborhoods to encourage families to patronize the business.

There were occasions when some patron would get out of line and this would require immediate action on the part of the bartender. He would grab the inebriated customer by the collar and seat of his britches and escort him out the nearest exit. One such patron had the misfortune of being hit by a speeding car. He landed on the soft grass sod and received only minor bruises.

We had a principal at junior high school who was "hell on wheels" on discipline. He was gassed during WWI while serving with the expeditionary forces in France.

For some minor rule infraction, for which I don't remember the details, I was sent to the principal's office to be disciplined. Mr. Hanes shoved me over his rolltop desk and bellowed at me like a bull. He didn't touch me but he scared the daylights out of me. I made up my mind then that I would not violate any more rules as long as I was in junior high.

While visiting in Pittsburgh one cold winter day, I noticed a crowd of people gathered in one of the empty buildings in the downtown area. I entered the building and saw some character shouting from a makeshift podium. The building was unheated and the temperature was near freezing.

This clown didn't have a shirt on and he was showing off his suntanned physique. he was spouting off about the merits of some famous elixir he was selling. People were buying this stuff as fast as his handlers could dispense it to the excited crowd. I wanted to buy a bottle but I didn't have the price of a 5 cent hot-dog.

Every year or so the circus would come to a nearby town. I often wished I had the price of admission. Once in a while I would get into the free midway area and listen to the barkers give their spiel. I was always fascinated by the unusual characters like the half-man/half-woman, the bearded lady and the two-headed gorilla.

The brass band would always be brought out to entertain the crowd while they introduced the beautiful ladies doing their fan dance. All these performers would come from the South Sea islands or some other remote place of the world.

Another unusual incident I remember was reported in the McKeesport daily newspaper. A young couple was driving home from a night at the local theater. Near the edge of town they saw a young lady standing on the sidewalk apparently waiting for someone.

She was dressed in a beautiful white gown and looked radiant as they approached her with the headlights revealing her beauty. They stopped and recognized her as a neighbor they hadn't seen in quite a while. The couple gave her a ride and let her out at their home since she said she would walk the rest of the way.

The next day the couple called and told the young lady's parents that they had given their daughter a ride home and told them how beautiful she looked. Her parents said that their daughter had died a couple of years ago.

The young couple assured the parents they were not mistaken and it must have been a miracle. Whether we believe in miracles or not, they do happen in some of the most unusual ways.

I also believe in guardian angels and I've called on mine many times.

RIDE TO FORTUNE DIDN'T LAST LONG
Sunday, June 18, 1995

Graduation from high school was certainly one of the highlights of a teenager born and raised in the steel mill country near Pittsburgh, PA during the Great Depression. How well I remember when I graduated from Duquesne High School in 1936. There were approximately 350 students in my class.

Our commencement speaker was a member of our school board and was one of the few affluent people of our town. I remember the last sentence of his speech as if it happened yesterday.

"All you students will go out into the real world and make your mark."

I thought to myself "Oh yeah! Our biggest challenge will be to survive."

The 1931 Chevrolet that I bought with my lottery winnings was going to be my ticket to better times. A couple buddies of mine and I decided to go to the East Coast to find our fortune. With about $30 we headed East with our exact destination unknown.

We traveled on US Highway 22, which was the most scenic route. It also proved to be the most treacherous route. Trucks were having problem climbing some of the mountains when they would get overheated. The drivers would park on the narrow shoulder of the road and go look for a creek to replenish the radiator water lost from overheating. There was no Prestone those days.

We didn't have that problem with our Chevy because we would stop at the top of the mountains and let things cool off. Time was no problem with us since we had no schedule to worry about.

At mealtime we would usually stop at some town along our route and buy groceries and make sandwiches. We would also stop at some fruit stand and talk the owner into donating some of the fruit that had been bruised but still edible.

We had a picnic everyday. At night we slept in the car. It was somewhat uncomfortable but in the morning we could get up and stretch and take all the kinks out. Then we would drive until we found a creek so that we could wash and freshen up.

About the third day we were nearing Darby, PA. We planned to stop there since my brother and sisters were staying at an orphanage there. Mother died when I was 13 years old and dad tried to keep the family together with the help of Aunt Mary.

The burden proved to be too great for all concerned so the three youngest children were placed in an orphanage. The three oldest children managed to stay with friends and relatives. I was next to the oldest and I stayed with my Aunt Mary. We arrived at the orphanage one afternoon and got to see my brother and sisters for a few minutes. They had strict rules that prevented me from disturbing their routine for long visits. I was very glad to see my brother and sisters since I hadn't seen them for a couple of years.

While there we managed to work for the orphanage for three or four days. We were paid 50 cents a day. I went to work for the plumber who was a full-time employee. Pat wasn't paid much but he did have a place to stay with room and board. Pat enjoyed a good cold beer so he would have me take him into town each evening. My buddies were given other laboring jobs and they envied me for the relatively soft job that I had. One of them decided the work was too much for him so he hitch-hiked home.

About the fifth day, we left hoping to find that pot of gold at the end of the rainbow. I had the address of some of my relatives who lived in New Jersey. We managed to find three of my kinfolk and we stayed with each for a couple of days. We were treated like long lost kinfolk are treated but we didn't want to over stay our visit.

After our visits with the kinfolk we headed for the New Jersey coast. We arrived at some resort area with a beautiful sandy beach. We laid around for a few days soaking up the sun and enjoying ourselves. I had a few extra dollars that the kinfolk had given me so we could afford to have fun in the sun.

On our way home we were already making plans for our next trip. We were dreaming of someday in the not too distant future to head for the West Coast. "Go West young man," was the cry of the pioneers and we wanted to join their ranks.

LESSONS LEARNED IN CIVILIAN CORPS
Sunday, October 22, 1995

My tour of duty in the Civilian Conservation Corps began the summer of 1936. I was a mere 18 years old, full of ambition and ready to conquer the world.

I reported to camp at Columbus, NE with my buddy and was issued army-type clothes and khaki uniforms. Later that summer we were issued olive drab uniforms.

It didn't take us long to get acquainted with the other fellows in the barracks that would be our home for the foreseeable future.

One of the guys asked me if I ever put on the gloves. I didn't want to be branded a pansy, so I said I had boxed a time or two. This was a terrible mistake because I was required to box a couple of rounds with a middleweight pug that evening.

He slapped me around a bit before I could get a punch in and he eased up when he saw that I was no match for him. Fortunately he took an interest in me and asked me to join him in running every evening for the next few weeks. He turned out to be a good friend.

Some weeks later, a circus came to town and several of us went to take in the sights. A boxing ring was set up and a rough-looking dude with the circus would take on all comers. One of our guys volunteered to go three rounds with this pro and bets were made by all the observers, including some of our guys.

Our man was not much of a match for this pro, but he let our guy get in a few licks to make it look good. When the match was over, the pro divided the entire proceeds of $8.75, giving our guy half. That was big money during those lean Depression years.

The annual county fair was held on the fair grounds adjacent to our camp. They had the usual judging of animals, home canned garden items and various crafts. They also had a race track with horse racing every afternoon.

I had never been at a race track before, so I thought I would invest $2 of my $5 monthly allowance on a race. My horse came in second and I was about to throw my ticket away when an acquaintance checked my ticket and told me I had won $4. I had played my horse to "show" and that's what it did. You don't have to be stupid to win at racing, but sometimes it helps.

Another annual event was the corn husking contest. It was held each year when the corn was ready to harvest. These events were promoted by local farmer groups and also hybrid corn seed promoters. Plots of ground were laid out in the spring and with the cooperation of the landowners, certain type seeds and fertilizer were used.

The corn would be irrigated to promote a very good yield for the contest. Rows of corn would be cleared so that a wagon could be driven through the long rows. Each contestant would be provided with a wagon with a backboard.

The contestants had contraptions tied to their wrists that contained a very sharp bladed instrument. With this device, the contestant would make one swipe at the corn and the husk would be cut and an ear of clean corn would be grabbed and heaved into the wagon. All this was done in a fraction of a second.

The contest would last about 2-1/2 hours and the wagons would be filled by this time. The corn would be weighed and penalties were assessed for any husks that were in the wagon. Prizes were awarded to the top three contestants, plus a good bit of publicity in the local papers and farm journals.

Back at camp, the most important event would be mail call. Many of the guys were homesick and mail from home was a great morale booster. A few of the guys had girlfriends who would write letters almost daily. Some of the guys rarely received mail from home.

There was one lad by the name of Shellenberger who was from a very poor family and never received mail. Each day he would be the first at mail call. I really felt sorry for him since he would always say that maybe tomorrow he would get a letter. Shelly (his nickname) could barely read or write, so I imagine his folks couldn't read or write. What a sad situation.

During the winter we would be assigned duties as night watchman and fireman. The barracks and other buildings were heated by pot-bellied stoves. I took my turn and got instructions from Shelly, who was getting off his shift. I was reminded to check all the stoves every two hours and to add coal if necessary.

I was told to be quiet while working the officer's quarters. It seems their stove smoked a lot more than the others. About the second round I made to their quarters, the place was filled with smoke. I heard the officers coughing and gagging, so I left their door open to get some fresh air in the room and stirred the coal up to get the flames started again. I finally got things under control and got out of their quarters before they realized what happened.

The most important chore the night watchman had was to get the cook stoves hot by 5:00 a.m. so the cooks could start breakfast. Their stoves were also fired with coal.

I made a terrible mistake by taking a short nap in the kitchen one early morning. It was 4:30 a.m. when I awoke and the fires were practically out. I used an old trick that the cooks used. I poured cooking oil on the half-smothered coal and apparently overdid it.

The flame shot out about four feet. It singed my eyebrows and I thought I was going blind. Well, I got over that and I knew that wouldn't happen again. I did get the stove hot enough for the cooks to prepare breakfast on time.

I blame all this on Shellenberger, since he was the one who taught me about keeping the home fires burning. He left for a weekend visit to his folk's home after he got off duty that night, so I didn't have an opportunity to chew him out.

Shelly always brought some goodies from home and I enjoyed them very much. He also brought back his parent's favorite remedy for sinus problems. It was skunk oil. If that didn't clear your head, you were doomed anyway.

I learned many lessons during my year in the Civilian Conservation Corps and found that hard work was the best experience any teenager can have. We didn't have time to get into trouble after a good workout in the fields.

We were indebted to President Franklin D. Roosevelt for the civilian Conservation Corps program that helped many families and their sons during the Great Depression.

WE MUST REMEMBER REASON FOR CELEBRATION
Sunday, December 24, 1995

Christmas during the 30s was a joyous occasion we all looked forward to as we do today. However, the birth of the Christ child was the reason for all the celebration. Today it seems that the gift giving takes precedence over the religious aspects of this holy day.

Growing up in the steel mill country near Pittsburgh, PA was different during this holiday. Some of the churches had services on Christmas Eve and church bells would ring reminding all to celebrate the birth of the Christ child. Many of the churches celebrated only on Christmas day when bells would ring again throughout the morning.

Duquesne, like most of the towns in the area, had many immigrants from the "Old Country." Church services were conducted in the language of their homeland. We didn't refer to churches as Protestant or Catholic. They were the German church, the Slovak church, the Hungarian church, the Russian church and others.

Most of the immigrants had large families and during the Great Depression, feeding of the family took priority over everything else. This was probably one of the reasons that gift giving was for the more affluent folks. Every ethnic group had its favorite foods to serve during the holiday.

We looked forward to having kalaches filled with various jams, ground-up walnuts, flavored cottage cheese, sweetened poppyseed and several other homemade fillings. Our parents never used recipes for these ethnic foods. Each generation would teach the children how to cook and bake these mouth-watering foods.

I remember one Christmas, while window shopping I saw a beautiful brush and comb set at a local store. The beautiful display case had velvet backing and it really caught my eye. I gazed at it a longtime and wondered if one day I could buy this as a Christmas gift for my mother.

I was only 12 years old and it was in the midst of the Depression and I knew it would take a miracle for this to happen. I never told anybody about this because I wanted it to be a secret until I could afford to buy it. This dream didn't come to pass since my mother died the following year, a few days before Christmas.

As years went by I celebrated Christmas at home with my Aunt Mary and her family. I lived with her until I left home years later.

The first time I was away from home for Christmas was in 1936. I was stationed in Madison, NE with the Civilian Conservation Corps. A few days before Christmas I developed a chronic case of tonsillitis and was sent to an Army medical facility at Fort

Crook, NE near Omaha. An Army surgeon operated on me the old fashioned way.

The surgeon seated me in a dentist type chair and said, "open your mouth wide and it will be over in a few minutes." It got a little more involved than that, but I managed to survive. It was a couple of days before Christmas and all I could do was look out the window and watch the soldiers hiking in the snow. This was the first time I remember being homesick. The song *I'll Be Home for Christmas* had more meaning for me after this experience.

In January 1941 Uncle Sam called me to serve in the armed forces for one year. Before the year was up, Pearl Harbor was bombed and the year was extended for the duration. All furloughs were canceled. I had 11 months service and due a furlough in December.

About the 15th of December we received word that the Army relented and I did get my leave and was home for Christmas. I was the happiest soldier in town. I enjoyed this Christmas, just being home with family and friends. I didn't get any gifts, but being home for Christmas was all the gift I wanted.

Our Army unit was sent to Europe in September 1944. We were in combat in Germany near the Holland border during Christmas 1944. I gave gifts to all the men in my section. The gifts were some of my personal possessions that I wrapped with paper from a package from home. It was a Christmas that I'll long remember. All we prayed for was to see another Christmas.

The war finally ended in May 1945 and we were assigned occupation duties until the war with Japan ended with the dropping of the two atom bombs in Hiroshima and Nagasaki in August 1945.

I was on the high seas during Christmas 1945 in a Victory ship when a terrible storm forced us to change course to avoid as much of the storm as possible. We hoped and prayed we would live through it. We finally landed on New Year's Day 1946 several hundred miles south of New York, which was our original destination.

I celebrated Christmas in January 1946 with my wife and daughter who I hadn't seen in almost two years. This was the happiest Christmas I can remember. I haven't missed Christmas with my family since then and I thank God for all the Christmases since coming home from the war.

I wish for all to enjoy this Christmas and may all the choicest blessings be yours this holiday season.

CENTERPIECE USUALLY BIG, FAT HEN
November 28, 1996

We celebrate Thanksgiving annually the fourth Thursday of November. This date was established as the official date of the national holiday during the time Franklin Delano Roosevelt was president.

The first Thanksgiving was celebrated by the Pilgrims in 1621. William Bradford was governor of Plymouth Colony at the time. The Pilgrims suffered the previous winter from the severe cold and lack of food and other essentials necessary for survival. They also suffered casualties from unfriendly Indians in the area.

Governor Bradford made peace with the Wampanaq tribe and invited them to a three-day festival. The harvest was sufficient enough to carry the Pilgrims through the coming winter. Wild game and crops that were recently harvested were shared with the Indians.

The Pilgrims turned to God in gratitude for sparing them from illness and death. They proclaimed a feast of Thanksgiving to God for his provident care.

We now celebrate Thanksgiving by inviting our family and friends to enjoy the turkey dinner, sage dressing, cranberry salad, sweet potatoes, pecan pies and all the other home-cooked foods of the season. We rarely admit that we are giving thanks to God for the bounty and abundance that he has provided.

There were subsequent Thanksgiving celebrations by the Pilgrims, but there seemed to be little fanfare compared to the original Thanksgiving celebration.

During the depression, only the affluent had the means to celebrate the traditional Thanksgiving Day with turkey and all the trimmings. There were very few affluent people during these times. We felt very fortunate if we could afford a fat hen.

Those rare occasions a live hen was purchased from the local market and kept overnight in the basement under a No. 2 washtub that was raised just enough to get air to the hen. The first order of business Thanksgiving morning was to kill and dress the hen (actually the hen was undressed) and cook it in the oven. Plenty of dressing was made and of course, the hen was stuffed with the best home-made dressing that you could afford.

There were times when Thanksgiving dinner consisted of very little meat of any kind. Canned vegetables from the garden usually was the main dish. We usually had home-baked bread and pastries since Aunt Mary managed to save enough flour for this special feast.

The first Thanksgiving complete with turkey, dressing and all the other goodies that I remember was during my time in the Civilian Conservation Corps (generally known as CCC Camp). After graduation from high school in 1936 I was given the opportunity to join the CCC.

I was roaming the country with a buddy and we happened to be in Neligh, NE. We found out that the county had not used up its quota for the CCC Camp and we qualified and were immediately sent to a camp nearby.

After a year in the CCC Camp, I returned back home to Duquesne, PA. I don't remember having turkey at Thanksgiving at home. It seemed that the "big fat hen" was the choice for Thanksgiving dinner. Since we didn't have refrigerators we couldn't preserve the leftovers more than a day or so. The big fat hen was much cheaper than the smallest turkey that was available.

After I was drafted in the Army in January 1941, I spent several Thanksgivings working for Uncle Sam. The Army believed in the traditional Thanksgiving meal of turkey, dressing and all the trimmings that are part of the feast. I always enjoyed those feasts and looked forward to the next one.

The next Thanksgiving of note was in Germany in 1944. We had been in combat for a few weeks before Thanksgiving. General Eisenhower sent word to all commands that turkeys would be available to all units in combat on Thanksgiving day.

Our supply personnel made certain that turkeys were the ration for this holiday and it was up to each unit to get the meal to all men in their command. I managed to get a turkey leg and enjoyed it to the fullest.

We didn't have the formal turkey dinner, but that turkey leg was really appreciated. That was a whole lot better than the K-rations and C-rations that were the norm.

I'm looking forward to this Thanksgiving Day with our family and friends and we will give thanks to God for this bounty that we have the privilege to share.

BRUTAL WINTERS LED TO GOOD, CLEAN FUN
Sunday, March 9, 1997

Winters of long ago were brutal and long lasting in the foothills of the Alleghenies south of Pittsburgh, PA.

The prevailing westerly winds brought snow and bitter cold from the Great Lakes and Canada. Winter winds usually began their howling in the latter part of September and continued erratically until the end of March.

The first snow would usually arrive in early October and continue off and on until spring. I remember snow storms that would leave drifts four and five feet high on your sidewalks. It was my chore to shovel the snow from our doorway to the street before going to school.

School buses were unheard of and private vehicles were as rare as roses in December. Everyone walked to school even if the snow was knee deep. School never closed because of inclement weather. Our schools were about two miles from our house and we walked it every day.

There were no school lunch programs, so we all walked home for lunch to get that hot bowl of homemade soup. School let out for lunch at 11:45 a.m. and we had an hour and 15 minutes before the bell rang for classes to begin. That didn't give us any time to goof off during lunch hour. You had to hustle.

We all looked forward to 4:10 p.m. when school was dismissed, so we could enjoy the snow. There was a lot of friendly snowball throwing on the way home. The girls were always a good target, but they could defend themselves by throwing snowballs at the boys who were harassing them.

We enjoyed the snow and didn't mind the cold weather. To get an idea how cold it got, all you had to do was go to the front porch and bring in the quart of milk your milkman delivered sometime during the wee hours of the morning. The cream rose about four inches above the top of the milk bottle with the paper lid still in place at the top of the cream. That's cold folks.

After supper and when your chores were done, you could get your sled out of the basement and get ready for a couple hours of fun.

We lived near the outskirts of town and there was a pasture nearby that was an ideal place to sled ride. The terrain was sloped just enough to get your sled moving fast.

A street dead-ended at the edge of the pasture which was blocked off with posts spaced about four feet apart. I usually could make it between these posts without any trouble, but the extremely icy conditions prevented me from guiding the sled between the posts on one occasion.

I hit the post head on and was thrown a few feet. I must have hit the post with my chest because I couldn't get my breath for awhile. I didn't tell anyone for fear of not being allowed out to sled ride in the future. Fortunately, I was not seriously hurt. I could have been grounded for the rest of the winter.

I guess the most fun we had was bobsledding. About six of us would get together and build a bobsled. It was two-part sled with a design similar to the design used on semis.

The driver would sit in the front part of the sled and steer it with a makeshift steering wheel. The back end could accommodate about six guys. We would usually find a long hill that was suitable for bobsledding.

The fellow at the back end would give it a shove to start it down the hill and then would hop on. Because of all the weight we could pick up speeds about twice as great as an ordinary sled. We could really make the sparks fly as we passed over minor obstructions. We weren't going as fast as the speed of light, but we thought we were at times.

There was a good size pond nearby that froze over when temperatures got below zero, which happened quite often. All the neighbor kids and adults would come out with their ice skates and join in the fun. This frozen pond could accommodate a large number of folks without any indication of ice giving away.

On one occasion, some clown drove his 1932 Model A around the pond without breaking the ice. That ice was frozen solid for a depth of at least a couple of feet. We were lucky because we never had a casualty from the ice giving away.

This was pure honest-to-goodness real clean family type enjoyment. We didn't get involved in dope because we didn't know that such stuff existed. How wonderful it would be if this would be true today. Wouldn't this world be a better place to live?

CIVILIAN CONSERVATION CORPS HELPED FAMILIES IN TOUGH TIMES
Sunday, March 22, 1998

I was stationed in Columbus, NE in the Civilian Conservation Corps in 1936. President Roosevelt was responsible for the legislation that authorized the Corps.

There was a lot of controversy when this legislation was being considered because only low income families could qualify to send their sons to the CCC Camps. Everyone feared that all these men would automatically become soldiers in case of a military emergency.

The monthly pay of $30 was not much, but during those depression days it was considered to be a small fortune. Five dollars of the $30 was retained for personal items and necessities and the remaining $25 was sent back home to the family. Those checks were a blessing to thousands of families who had sons in the CCC Camps.

I enjoyed my tour of duty in the camp and made a lot of friends. I guess I enjoyed the three nutritious meals more than anything. If you ever had to miss a few meals and wonder when you would have your next meal you would understand the full impact of this situation.

Our day would start at 5:30 a.m. when the bugler would wake us with his military wake up call. The first thing we did was grab our toothbrushes, shaving cream, etc. and dash to the washroom in the building about 100 yards from our barracks. In the summertime we probably had only our underwear on, but in the cold winter we probably had our overcoats over our long johns. Dashing through the snow in sub-zero weather would wake one up in a hurry.

By breakfast time, 7:00 a.m., you had your bed made up and the barracks mopped and cleaned. Military discipline was necessary to keep everything orderly when there are 50 men living in the same barracks with you. Discipline never hurt anybody and it certainly could make a mature person out of you in a hurry.

Breakfast was one of my favorite meals. The menu always included cereal, bacon, eggs, toast, juice, milk and coffee. Occasionally fried potatoes were served. Our cooks did everything they could to see that we got a hearty breakfast. The full time baker usually had biscuits, doughnuts and other pastries for the breakfast and evening meals.

We were fortunate to have Sandy, our baker, in our camp. The salaries of our cooks and baker were $36 a month. All these people were members of the Civilian Conservation Corps.

Our first sergeant kept a duty roster and everyone except supervisory personnel would be eligible for KP, dining room orderly and night watchman. These duties were posted on the bulletin board daily.

I enjoyed the job of dining room orderly most of all. This duty consisted of setting all the tables and cleaning up after each meal. You also had the opportunity of testing the food before meals were served. When grapefruit halves where served, usually there were several left on the tables after breakfast. I gathered them all up and squeezed the juice into a large container and sipped on it all morning.

The dining room orderly's job included the making of sandwiches to be taken out to the field where the crews were working. Peanut butter and jelly sandwiches and baloney was usually served. Apples or oranges were usually included in the lunch. Ice water was about the only drink that was furnished.

The Soil Conservation Service was responsible for the design of all work to be carried out by the Corps. They secured contracts from the farmers and other property owners where the work was carried out. The Corps furnished the personnel for the survey crews to lay out contours and other work to be performed by the Corps.

The majority of our work was intended to take care of the erosion problems that were washing the land. The severe drought of the 30s caused land to be blown away by dust storms. Our job was to save the soil for future generations.

There were many camps in the US that did all kinds of work for the Soil Conservation Service. Numerous roads were built on federal lands. Thousands of acres of trees were planted. Underbrush was cleared where trees could start growing again. Small lakes were built where deer, turkey and other wild game could survive during the drought that plagued the country during the 30s. Many farms were saved from serious erosion problem.

Back at camp during the evening we would sit around and reminisce about our childhood days back home. Most of the fellows wrote letters to folks back home. Some wrote letters each evening to girlfriends they hadn't seen in months. We all went to mail call after supper in hopes of getting letters from home.

Many years have passed since the Civilian Conservation Corps did all the important work to save our soil. Millions of acres of land was saved for future generations. We are still reaping rewards from the work that was carried out by the CCC. I am glad I had some small part in this worthwhile project.

INTEREST IN PONIES BEGAN DURING CHILDHOOD DAYS
Sunday, June 14, 1998

My first experience with ponies was during a vacation when I was five years old. We were visiting kinfolk who owned a country store in New Jersey.

They had a Shetland pony that roamed the pasture adjacent to the store. Since the pony was gentle, I got permission to ride it in the pasture. I felt like a real cowboy riding the range.

I fell in love with the pony and asked the folks if I could take it home. They promised me they would send it to my home by rail as soon as they could make the necessary arrangements. After I got home, I anxiously waited for my pony to arrive.

Everyday when the train came through our town I would hope that my pony was on that train. I waited a long time and the pony never arrived. It took me a long time to get over this disappointment.

The next time I had the opportunity to ride a pony was during a school picnic when I finished the first grade. School picnics were always held at Kennywood Park, which is about four miles from our home in Duequesne, PA.

All schools were given complimentary tickets for the rides at the park. Each student would get 10 tickets that would be used for most of the rides. Pony rides required five tickets, so I used mine for two pony rides.

It was a real thrill to ride around the quarter-mile track. We couldn't afford to buy any tickets since we were in the midst of the Great Depression.

Many years went by before I had another opportunity to ride a horse again. I was stationed at Fort Sam Houston, near San Antonio during WWII, I heard about all the famous dude ranches in the Hill Country that was located about 40 miles from San Antonio.

My private's military pay limited my activities to trips to San Antonio by bus to the nearest pub. The next couple of years I finally received promotions and pay increases.

In August 1942 I was transferred to Paris, TX to help organize the 102nd Infantry Division at Camp Maxey. A few of my Army buddies invited me to go eat steak at a popular restaurant across Red River in Oklahoma.

After dinner, which included a couple of beers I left the restaurant to get a little air while my buddies were finishing up their liquid rations. It was a dark night and I stood there admiring the stars in the sky.

I heard a clomping of hoofs coming down the road. It turned out to be a large Belgian-looking horse without a rider. The horse slowed down when he saw the lights from the restaurant.

He appeared to be gentle so I jumped on and thought I would take a short ride. I grabbed the makeshift reins and tried to steer him off the road. He decided to go straight for the door to the restaurant but was stopped because he couldn't bend his head enough to get through the door.

I jumped off the horse before he got to the door. I gave the horse a gentle nudge and he took off into the darkness.

Since we were new to the community of Paris we were invited to a USO dance by the local ladies organization. I met a charming young lady at the dance who I eventually dated for several months. We married in April 1943, even though we knew I would be going overseas as soon as the troops were adequately trained for combat. Sometime later I managed to get a leave of absence and we decided to spend a weekend at a dude ranch in the Hill Country.

The main activity of the ranch was horseback riding. They gave me a beautiful black horse to ride and placed me at the rear of the group of about 20 horses. We were riding at a leisurely pace and I let the reins get a little slack, which turned out to be a terrible mistake.

The horse took off like he was struck by lightning and headed for a grove of trees. I tried to grab the reins when I saw my horse headed for some long-hanging limbs. Through some miracle I managed to slide to the side of the horse, hanging on for dear life.

The horse ducked his head to keep the limbs from tearing off his head. I managed to get through the grove of trees with only a few scratches.

The ranch hands finally caught up with my horse and helped to slow him down. I finally grabbed the reins and took control of my fleet-footed horse. One experience like this should last for a lifetime.

I had no more opportunities to go horseback riding until the war was over in Germany in May 1945. We were doing occupation duty and had plenty of time for organized sports and other leisure-time activities. Our military commanders relaxed our Army rules since we had just finished defeating the Germans and we deserved some well-earned relaxation and recreation.

The German Cavalry released their horses after the war to roam the countryside. The local farmers rounded up these horses and used them to plow their fields and do other chores.

We found out that our troops were interested in horseback riding, so we decided to round up some horses that were turned loose by the German army. Three of us got a jeep and rode out into the country to find these horses.

Everytime we saw a farmer with a horse, we would check to see if it had military markings. Through an interpreter we would tell the farmer that we would borrow his ill-gotten horse and would bring it back when we got through with it.

We would give the farmer a receipt, which he requested and would sign some fictitious officer's name, which satisfied him. None of these horses were returned while we were in occupation.

We finally rounded up 25 horses and hired a former young Hungarian cavalry solider to care for them. A roster was prepared and anyone who wanted to ride was scheduled for the time that was convenient for him to ride. The program was very popular and we continued it until we were relieved of occupation duties and headed back to the good old USA.

The only interest I have in horses now are the ones that race at Hot Springs and Bossier. I enjoy thoroughbred racing and I'll let the jockeys do the horseback riding.

MILITARY EXPERIENCES
JANUARY 1941-MARCH 1946

OUR FIRST EXPERIENCE IN A COMBAT ZONE

Our first headquarters established inside of Germany was at Palenberg which is located a short distance from the Holland border. The Germans had been forced out of this area by the relentless drive by our allied armies. The fortifications of the famed Siegfried Line were being breached by our advancing troops.

Tank traps surrounded the area. Civilians young and old including children were forced to help dig trenches for additional tank traps. Foxholes were also being dug by the civilians. All displaced persons, political prisoners and others were also used to dig these trenches under the watchful eyes of the German military.

Most of the people fled from their homes as our armies approached. The few who hesitated to leave were forced out of their homes by the military. It didn't pay to resist because the punishment would have been brutal beatings or even death.

Our infantry units were some distance ahead of our headquarters and our artillery units were located at strategic areas to support the infantry units.

There were several 155 Howitzers located in the immediate area of our headquarters. These 155s could hit targets considerably farther than the 105s of our 380th FA Battalion. Our 105s were accurate at about five miles.

The 155s could be heard screaming overhead if you were anywhere near these guns. It was a good feeling to know they were going out instead of coming in.

There was an unusual amount of military vehicles, tanks and other military equipment moving up to the front as we settled into our headquarters. We never knew what was going on until a day or so after it happened. Sometimes it was days after certain battles were fought before we were aware of what happened. We were aware of what was going on in our immediate area and we seldom knew what the big picture was until much later.

An afternoon in the park in San Antonio with Jim Resta, 1941

We were not allowed to write home about our specific activities because of the secrecy involved in military operations. However, newspapers back home would print stories the day after things happened. We would get mail from home that kept us informed of the activities of the military that was supposedly secret.

Our headquarters in Palenberg was a partially destroyed administrative building of a large coal mine operation. It was a much better place than living in a camouflaged tent or makeshift dugout.

We used lanterns for light to carry out our administrative duties. Mantles for these lanterns were not available through the military in our area so we sent home for these parts. The mantles were so delicate that they would fall apart with the least amount of movement. Fortunately, we found a supplier who was glad to fill our order for these items.

We prepared daily "morning reports" from information received from our units. We would receive messages by runners, radio communications and other methods. It was the responsibility of "first sergeants" to get information to us regarding sick reports, men hospitalized, wounded in action, killed in action, missing in action and anything else that required reporting.

Our first casualty was a member of the forward observer team at B Battery, 380th FA Battalion. The forward observer worked closely with the infantry companies and would relay firing directions to the battalion fire direction center. Adjustments would be made and relayed to the gun crews so that the enemy targets could be destroyed.

I don't remember the name of the forward observer who was hit by the German artillery but he was the first soldier of our battalion killed in action. In order to officially report "a killed in action" report, the body had to be identified by the graves registration unit.

A missing in action report had to be made until the body could be retrieved from the battlefield. Since incoming artillery was so devastating, it would take a day or more to get to the body. The missing in action report was misleading since it covered several conditions. Some men could have been temporarily lost from their unit for several days. Others could have been taken prisoner by the Germans. There were times when men were wounded and couldn't move until the medics found them.

The unsung heroes of the war were the medics, the first aid men assigned to the field artillery batteries and infantry companies saved a lot of lives by treating the wounded on the battlefield. Sulfa was the miracle drug of the 40s. It was used on all wounds (in powder form) and reduced infection dramatically. Doctors in rear echelon hospitals were amazed at how well wounds were treated by these medics.

Reports of casualties of members of your unit would be difficult to deal with. Reports of death were devastating and would make you feel numb. You couldn't realize how terrible war was until the first death of a member of your organization.

Many men had a difficult time getting over the death of a buddy. Some developed mental problems commonly called "Battle Rattle." Eventually most men would get over the initial shock but would never get hardened enough to forget these terrible experiences.

FROM THE ROER RIVER TO THE RHINE

About the last week of February 1945, we got orders to move our 102nd Infantry Division, Administrative Headquarters to Linnich, Germany. We were in a convoy of several 2-1/2 ton trucks making the trip in broad daylight. We were strafed by a lone German plane that made one pass at us and left in a hurry. Our machine guns were mounted near the top of the cab where it could revolve 360 degrees at any target. Several rounds were fired but we don't know if any actually hit the plane. Near the end of the war, we found German planes on the ground near air strips that had been shot full of holes.

After a few hours of stop and go driving, we reached our destination near Linnich. Our cooks set up the cooking gear in a wooded area and started to prepare our meal. Again, that lone German plane came out of the clouds and strafed us again. Our luck held out and we managed to get by again without any casualties.

By night time we managed to get to an abandoned building to set up our headquarters. The basement in these houses had tunnels leading from one basement to the other. There were several houses in the area and they all had tunnels from their basements to the next basements. At the end of the street there was a tunnel that went across the street to the row of houses on that side of the street.

The Germans had used these tunnels when they were defending the area near the Roer River. Our infantry had also used these basements since we found rations and blankets that they had left behind after they crossed the Roer River.

Our Air Force was very active in this area and we heard their planes roaring through the skies. They dropped tin foil strips similar to icicles used on Christmas trees. This was intended to foul up the radar that the Germans were using to track our Air Force planes. Our bombers dropped their auxiliary gas tanks in the area and the German civilians were cautioned to keep away from them because they may be booby-trapped. Well, it developed that the Germany military would retrieve these tanks since they did contain a small amount of airplane fuel. Fuel was a very scarce and precious item and the German military was badly in need of every drop of fuel.

After the Roer River crossing, our infantry and artillery moved north to Krefeld near the Rhine River. Our infantry had advanced so rapidly that many civilians were unable to flee across the Rhine River. The street cars were in operation as the infantry approached the various villages near the Rhine River.

The building that we stayed in was a former Nazi youth organization headquarters. There were all sorts of Nazi memorabilia which included various types of cameras. Everyone in our section got at least one camera. Some were lucky enough to get the famous "Leika" camera. I managed to get an old box camera that I used for a while. Sometime later I lost my camera during one of our frequent moves.

Ready for bayonet drill, Fort Sam Houston, 1941.

We eventually moved up to the Krefeld area near the Rhine River. Many civilians were still in the area since they were surprised by the fast moving infantry. Guards had to be posted in various areas in order to keep track of the civilians.

We moved into a partially bombed out building that was a former Nazi headquarters. Pictures of Hitler and other Gestapo characters were hanging on the walls of their meeting rooms. Some of the guys found all sorts of pictures of Nazis in uniform. Pictures of military trips, parades and other activities were also found by some of the guys.

There was a beautiful chandelier in one of the Nazi headquarters rooms that we really admired. Some of the guys thought they would take a ride on these chandelier by taking a running jump and grab the fixture and use it for a swing. This proved to be a lot of fun for a moment until we decided it was behavior unbecoming to an American soldier.

The post office was located on the ground floor of this building. Apparently the employees there were surprised at our fast moving military that they left in a hurry. All the money was still in the cash registers and all the packages sent to the German soldiers by their families were stacked untouched in the post office.

Most everyone got a handful of the German currency. We figured it was worthless and most of us just kept some for souvenirs. Some of the money was thrown out of the upper story windows and just watched it flutter to the ground.

When the war was over we found out that the German currency was still legal tender. We could use it to buy most anything that was available. However, most of the items of value were non-existent. Sometimes we had an opportunity to buy some jewelry through the black market. This was the beginning of the end of the infamous Nazi empire.

FROM FRANCE TO THE HOLLAND-GERMAN BORDER DURING WWII

Our trip from France to the Holland-German border in 2-1/2 ton trucks took a couple of days. There were 15-20 men complete with full-field equipment and rifles in each truck in the convoy. It was in early November 1944, when this trip was taking place. The scenery from the back-end of these GI trucks was as monotonous as expected.

We were issued K-rations for the trip and we looked forward to getting a break from riding those trucks. I remember stopping in Mastrich, Belgium, a relatively large town for a lunch break. There was a store nearby that was frequented by GIs that got our attention. We went in to see what was available in the way of food and we were disappointed. The only thing that they sold was an imitation ice cream made out of ice and other ingredients including coloring that didn't appeal to us.

We decided that our K-rations were about as good as we could have so we opened our K-rations and enjoyed our picnic lunch. Food was a very scarce item in several of the European countries. Belgium seemed to be better off than most since the Germans did very little looting in Belgium.

K-rations consisted of a small can of cheese, Spam, scrambled eggs and other similar items. Hard crackers and a small pack of cigarettes, four in a pack and occasionally a piece of bitter chocolate that was hard as a rock. All these items were packed in a cardboard box the size of a Cracker Jack box.

After lunch we were on our way again north to Holland and on to the German border. We arrived in the city of Heerlen, Holland after dark. We settled down in a school house over night and waited for further orders next morning. It was bitter cold riding in those 2-1/2 ton trucks and we were glad to get inside a building to get thawed out.

Blackout conditions existed in almost all areas of France, Belgium and Holland because of continuous aerial reconnaissance by the Germans. At night we could hear some brave soul clomping along in his wooden shoes on his way home from some necessary trip. Usually it was considered unsafe to be out during the hours of darkness. Windmills gave off a screeching noise that was frightening to hear at night until we got used to this awful noise.

We made arrangements with the local folks to wash our clothes and we were glad to have such a luxury available. Showers were also available at the local coal mining complex at no cost. People of Holland were so appreciative of our military that they wouldn't charge us for doing our laundry. Everyone had their favorite family to do these chores. We would give them candy, gum and other items received from home to show our appreciation.

Our chow lines were set-up on one of the streets in town and we would eat outdoors, weather permitting. The local children showed up at mealtime and the cooks would give them all the leftovers to take home to their families.

The children were taught English from the first grade on and we enjoyed talking to them. We even taught them songs that they managed to learn very quickly. These children were a constant reminder of our families back home. Most of the older folks couldn't speak English and we had a difficult time communicating with them.

Our infantry was already in combat and our artillery units were getting prepared to join them. After several days of combat we were given orders to move into the village of Palenberg, Germany. We set up our headquarters in an old coal mine administrative building that was damaged by bombings by our Air Force that was stationed in England.

As we were unloading our equipment, a German fighter plane strafed us with .50 caliber bullets before we knew what hit us. We ran inside the building and managed to escape without having anyone hurt. These fighter planes came out of the clouds at about 500 mph and you had very little time to react. Usually these planes would make one pass and then they were gone.

There were several artillery units in the area that were not involved in the strafing because of very effective camouflage that was used.

We set up our headquarters in this coal mine building and made this our home for the next few weeks. We used lanterns and candles for several days to carry out the essential administrative functions of our headquarters. We would get daily reports from our battalion headquarters by messenger or by other methods.

About once a week I would report to our battalion commander, Colonel Hannigan, to carry out some essential duties that he requested.

I would visit the five batteries of our battalion as often as necessary to pay the troops and take care of any problems they might have including their allotments to their families back home. It was of utmost importance to take care of any problems that affected the welfare of our fighting troops. The morale of our men was of utmost importance and we did everything possible to keep the morale at a high pitch.

Thanksgiving In Germany During WWII

The greatest morale booster during WWII in Europe was mail from home. Regardless of what the military commanders would tell the news media about morale in their units, it was mail from home that determined the status of the morale of the troops. Of course the military situation had some affect on troop morale.

Most of the mail coming from the States came by freighter. It usually took 30 days from the day it was mailed until the troops received it at mail call. Space on aircraft was too valuable to carry tons of mail, we were told. V-mail was finally introduced since too many complaints were being made about the poor mail service. V-mail was a letter that contained one sheet of thin paper that folded into an envelope. Some sort of photo method was used to make prints of these letters that reduced the volume to a fraction of the regular mail. Then this mail would qualify for air shipment. Many tons of mail was lost since many of our freighters were sunk by German submarines.

I would write a short letter each day and hope that it would eventually get to its destination. When situations required our movement, I would write the letters when we would finally settle down to our new location. Then I would write a letter for each day that I missed while we were on the move.

Because of the battle situations, mail call would be delayed until it was possible to get to the troops. Some time it would be several days between mail calls. When a package would arrive from home it would usually be crushed with some of the contents missing. We always shared the goodies with our buddies. I remember getting a two-pound hunk of hard salami from my sister that I really enjoyed. I shared about half with my buddies and put the rest in my knapsack. Salami was highly seasoned and it would keep indefinitely. In the evenings, when I would have hunger pangs, I would get my pocket knife out and cut off a piece of the salami and enjoy a midnight snack. That was a real treat.

Water was one of the essentials of surviving. As long as you were near a military unit that had kitchen facilities you could get your canteen filled. We were taught to use two halazone tablets in each canteen of water regardless where it came from. These tablets turned the water a soapy color but it would keep you from having various stomach ailments like diarrhea. The people who lived in these areas built up an immunity to these ailments. According to international agreements during war time, it was legal to poison the water provided that adequate signs were posted to let you know that the water was contaminated.

During combat you lose track of time and usually you don't know the day of the week. You certainly don't remember various holidays and there is nothing you could do to celebrate these occasions.

General Eisenhower decided that the troops should have special treatment on Thanksgiving Day regardless of the military situation. Turkey was to be furnished to all troops and all units were advised that turkey would be included in the rations for that day.

The weather on Thanksgiving Day was like a typical Thanksgiving Day back home. The temperature was in the 30s with a brisk wind blowing hard enough to require additional clothing to keep warm.

I was on my way to meet with my battalion commander, Col. Hannigan, since he requested my presence. I planned to get a turkey leg or some part of the turkey for my Thanksgiving dinner. Before I got to my destination, a GI in tears stopped me to tell me of a soldier who had been killed a day or so ago and his frozen body was lying on the ground next to a tank. I assured him that the graves registration personnel would be around to pick up the bodies in that area as soon as they could get to that area. I told him that the next of kin would be notified and a proper burial would be carried out by the military. After talking to him for a while he seemed to calm down so I continued my journey to meet my battalion commander.

I was humbled by this experience and was no longer interested in Thanksgiving dinner. I arrived at battalion headquarters and met with Col. Hannigan and made notes of things he wanted me to accomplish.

On the way back to my unit I couldn't help but think of that young soldier, probably in his teens, who was so moved by the horrors of war. Usually it takes several experiences before you overcome the initial fears that haunt you day and night. You never get totally over these feelings but somehow you manage to live with them.

The war continued for several more months and God spared me from being wounded or killed. I have many things to be thankful for and Thanksgiving has more meaning to me as the days go by.

ATROCITIES NEAR THE END OF WWII

The first week of April 1945, the allied troops started to cross the Rhine River. The armored units were leading the assault over the major highways leading to the Elbe River and on to Berlin. All the roads on either side of the main highways were bypassed and left for the infantry and other units to mop up.

It was difficult to determine whether any resistance would be met in any of these bypassed areas the infantry and artillery units met several die-hard Nazi divisions that were hell-bent on protecting their area from the allied troops. Many individual battles were fought and the Nazis were determined to save the "Fatherland" even though they knew the end was near.

Some of the German military units were not ready to die for "DER Fuhrer" started to surrender to the various individual units of our 102nd Infantry Division. Even though some vicious fighting was still going on in isolated areas, white surrender flags were coming out of hiding.

The German commanders were surrendering their individual battalion size units without advising their superiors in many cases. They were surrendering their troops to any officer that happened to be near by. They usually demanded to surrender to higher ranking officers but many times they would agree to surrender to whatever ranking officer was available.

One of our forward observers rode on the back end of a German officer's motorcycle to locate a ranking officer to surrender the German unit. Even non-commissioned officers led the German units to various allied headquarters to officially surrender.

Some individuals of our division were taken prisoner during all the confusion of the fast moving advance of our troops. Some of these troops would be held prisoner for a couple of days and then they would be released because the German's decided to surrender.

Sergeant Barlow and I managed to start down a road that we thought had been liberated and almost ran into a German unit. We immediately turned around and got out of the area leaving a trail of dust to cover our retreat.

Many times the prisoners were marched down the road single file following one of our military vehicles to temporary prisoner compounds. There was no need for guards since these prisoners were glad their part of the war was over.

The Germans feared the Russians because they knew that if they were captured by the Russians they would be sent to Siberia. The Russians were driving toward Berlin with their armored units but were still several miles further from Berlin than the allied troops.

Some of the allied troops had crossed the Elbe River which was about 40 miles from Berlin. These troops were pulled back to the Elbe River upon orders from higher headquarters. Our troops could have reached Berlin much sooner than the Russians but the order from General Eisenhower's Headquarters was to stop at the Elbe River. This decision was made months in advance by Winston Churchill, Joseph Stalin and F.D. Roosevelt at the Yalta Conference.

Politics always get in the way of intelligent decisions. At the Yalta Conference of the "Big Three" discussions were held about who was to enter Berlin first. It was decided that it would be tremendous morale booster if the Russian armies would enter this former city of Nazi world domination.

While the war was winding down a bit in our section of combat, our 405th Infantry Regiment located south of our units were running into Nazi units that were guarding the approaches to the city of Gardelagen. A very important airfield was located here and the Nazis planned to defend this strong point at all cost.

An all out offensive was planned and before it was put into action the commandant of the Gardelagen Garrison had lost all desire to defend the fatherlands. He was persuaded to surrender by our liaison officer in the area since he realized that defensive action would be futile.

The surrender was ill-timed because it interrupted the atrocity that was just being carried out by the Nazis. On the outskirts of town, a barn partially full of hay soaked with gasoline was set afire with 300 slave laborers inside that could not get out because of the Nazi guards shooting anyone who attempted to crawl out of the barn. Freshly dug common graves were found nearby which the Nazis planned to use to bury the charred bodies.

After further investigation 1,000 bodies of allied military prisoners had also been found murdered nearby. The citizens of Gardelagen were not aware of any atrocities being carried out and they were shocked at the barbaric treatment of these prisoners.

The men of my section and I visited Gardelagen and saw the smoldering bodies inside the barn. What a terrible barbaric atrocity! How can a human being do such an inhuman act?

General Keating, commanding general of the 102nd Infantry Division issued orders that the citizens of this town were charged with the responsibility of burying these murdered prisoners and that their graves would forever be kept as green as the memory of these unfortunate souls.

An appropriate sign was erected at this site to tell whoever visits this cemetery of the terrible atrocity that occurred on these hallowed grounds.

SERVING NATION IS A VALUABLE LESSON
Sunday, April 1996

Veterans Day always brings back memories of my military service during WWII.

The train ride on January 18, 1941 from the induction center in Pittsburgh to Fort Meade, MD was uneventful until some of the draftees produced their favorite beverage from their luggage. We had about 20 draftees in our car and most of them had a pretty good appetite for bourbon. The bottles were passed around.

We were traveling at night and didn't reach our destination until daybreak. The civilians in our coach didn't seem to mind all the chatter and singing that went on most of the night. People were very patriotic during that time. We had some pretty good singers in our group, so maybe they enjoyed it.

After an hour or so of sleep, the conductor woke us up and told us we were nearing our destination. We got our belongings together and waited for the train to stop.

It was bitter cold with temperatures in the 30s as we neared the exit ramps. I suddenly realized that I had on only one shoe. I ran back to my coach seat for my other shoe as the train started to pull out of the station. The conductor was ready to throw me off as I hobbled to the entrance with shoe in hand.

I had to jump off as the train started to pick up speed. I fell to the ground; nothing was hurt but my pride. I guess the bourbon numbed my backside, which was bruised from the fall.

We spent the next three days taking aptitude tests so we could be placed in units where our experience would be helpful to the military. The only other duty was roll call in the wee hours of the morning. I would dash out with only my underwear and overcoat on and freeze during roll call. That 30 degree weather with 20 mph wind would wake you up in a hurry.

After three days of aptitude testing, we were all called out for another roll call. I assumed we would be separated and sent to various Army camps based on the results of the many tests. After roll call we were notified that all of us were assigned to an infantry division and would be leaving for Fort Sam Houston in San Antonio, TX.

Only the Army could dream up this waste of talent after all the aptitude tests for three days. It didn't take us long to realize that there were only two ways to do things: "The right way and the Army way."

After a two-day train ride, we arrived at Fort Sam Houston and were assigned to Dodd Field for basic training. We were housed in four-man tents with a pot bellied stove in each.

There was a boardwalk to a large airplane hangar that was used as our dining facility. Another boardwalk was built to our outdoor washroom and privy. The reason for the boardwalks was the blackland mud that would bog you down, cling to your boots, make you six inches taller and unable to move very much.

The corporal who was on duty came to our tent the first morning and told me to report for KP duty at 5:00 a.m. He told me to hang my drawers in the doorway of my tent so he could find me in the morning. I immediately obeyed his order since he waited for me to act. Later I retrieved my drawers so they couldn't find me in the morning.

I got up about 6:00 a.m. that morning and went for breakfast. After eating I walked around the back door and went into the kitchen. The KPs were all busy washing pots and pans and doing other chores. I grabbed the coal bucket and shovel and started to remove the ashes from the cook stoves that were fired with coal. I felt lucky to have pulled this off without anyone being the wiser. Getting caught could have been detrimental to my military career.

Our corporal in charge was a typical regular Army soldier who had several years of service. He looked every bit a solider and knew how to treat us draftees. We responded and admired him and would be honored to go into battle with him as our leader. He was a rare breed and proud to be a soldier. We were proud of our 12-weeks military training and we proved it at our final inspection.

After passing the final tests, we were assigned to the famous 2nd Infantry Division stationed at Fort Sam Houston. We were congratulated by our 23rd Infantry Regimental Commander and were told that we were a part of the most famous infantry division in the US Army. Our division received numerous decorations and honors for heroic performances in WWI.

We fell into the Army routine in a few days and learned to adjust without too much difficulty. After a few weeks we were assigned guard duty. There were 24-hour shifts with two hours duty and two hours of relief.

My first assignment was "chasing prisoners." I reported to the post prison and was assigned three prisoners to clean up certain areas and other miscellaneous duties.

I gave the command to "forward march" and the prisoners started to run. I hollered "halt" and they stopped immediately. I had a riot-type shotgun that was to deter any attempt to run off. I gave the prisoners specific instructions on what to do and told them that their behinds would be full of buckshot if they misbehaved.

I never fired my weapon, but I knew if I had to, I would. We were told that we would have to serve their time if our prisoners got away. I didn't have any plans to do such a foolish thing.

Army discipline taught me a lot about life. I can assure you that you can mature in a hurry. Our present generation is missing out on the greatest education one can get. Every high school graduate should be required to serve his country for a minimum of one year. Then he will have earned his rights granted by the US Constitution.

LIFE IN INFANTRY TURNED BOYS INTO MEN DURING WWII
Sunday, June 22, 1996

Patriotism was an honorable thing during the period 1940-46. Most every red-blooded young American, with few exceptions, was proud to be drafted and serve his country. Many young women volunteered for the various military services and served honorably during WWII.

The infantry was one branch of the service that lived up to the motto of many military schools: "Send us the boy and we will send home a man." No truer words were ever spoken.

I was drafted in January 1941 and served in an infantry division for more than five years. The infantry believed in total discipline which you appreciated as you grew older.

The military believed in providing you with a hearty breakfast. After breakfast you would get into formation and march to the parade grounds for morning calisthenics. Then you would stack your rifles military style and remove your shirt, weather permitting and start a half hour of strenuous exercises.

The pushups were done about 30 times and that would leave you limp and exhausted. There were no quitters. The side-straddle hop was a real killer. Done about 40-50 times in 90 percent humidity, it would test your endurance - especially if you had a night out on the town the night before.

I enjoyed marching more than anything else in the service. Usually about twice a month we would march to the parade ground where the famous 9th Infantry Regimental Band would play Sousa's famous military marches. If this wouldn't make you swell with pride, you were not totally alive.

We had one solider in our company that must have had two left feet. He could not keep in step with or without music. His platoon sergeant would march alongside of him and count cadence - left-right - to no avail.

He was always placed at the extreme end of the formation so he wouldn't foul up the others who kept perfect step with or without music. This soldier was eventually transferred out to some other unit for further training.

Many dignitaries from foreign countries visited the US during WWII. It seems that they all managed to come to Fort Sam Houston to view our training methods.

A parade was always scheduled for these visits and we marched to the music of the 9th Infantry Regimental Band regardless of the weather. I loved marching, but with 100 degree-plus heat and class A uniform with tie, it was not my favorite pastime. After we marched past the reviewing stand, we would be given the command to "double time" and that would really make your day.

Payday weekends were a special time for the old timers who loved to gamble. The dice table was set up behind the barracks after dark and the gamblers would start to gather. The games would go on most of the night.

Returning from town one night, I stopped to observe the dice game behind our barracks. I hid in the shadows where I could not be seen. I saw Sgt. Reed, my platoon sergeant, switch dice. Using these loaded dice a few times could win you a bundle. Of course, if you got caught you could get your head bashed in.

I was not a gambler and didn't care to get involved in these games. My private's pay of $30 a month was not enough to take care of the very essentials of life in the service. Eventually, I did get some promotions and pay increases, but gambling was not one of my priorities.

I guess every Army unit had its share of troublemakers. We had a Pvt. Robertshaw who was always getting into trouble everytime he went to town. The MPs would bring him in or our company com-

mander would give him the maximum punishment authorized by Summary Court Martial which was seven days of extra duty.

During peacetime, this soldier would have been given a discharge without honor. The military services were

Testing my rifle in Germany 1944.

instructed to salvage every person possible because of the need for soldiers during the world crises situation.

A few weeks after the last episode of discipline problems with this character, the company commander received good news. The Army was rounding up troublemakers and shipping them to some remote islands off the coast of Alaska for some special duty.

Capt. Hinch, our company commander, had to wait three days before this transfer took place. In order to make sure Pvt. Robertshaw would be present and available for this transfer, the company captain had to take some serious action.

He called on Pvt. Lorenso, a well-respected boxer in our company to keep Pvt. Robertshaw in tow until his transfer. All went well and the transfer took place without any trouble. Pvt. Lorenso was rewarded with a 10-day furlough for all his efforts.

We had another character in our company who was born and raised in Brooklyn and he apparently was never disciplined at home. He had a habit of wanting to talk back to his superiors. Of course he had enough sense to shut up when told to do so, otherwise he would have been spending his time in the brig and eventually be discharged dishonorably.

We had about 50 Yankees (New Yorkers) in our company and most of them were good soldiers. I made friends with several of them and we would go to a good Italian restaurant about once a month to eat spaghetti.

Unfortunately, there are people in all walks of life who do not want to live by the laws of the land and they must be disciplined so that all other people can enjoy peace and freedom guaranteed by the Constitution.

GI BUDDIES FIND TIME FOR RECREATION WHILE STATIONED IN TEXAS
Sunday, September 29, 1996

Draftees during WWII were paid $21 a month for the first four months service. If you didn't get into trouble during that time, your pay was increased to $30 a month. Big deal!

The military furnished your clothes and most all of the necessities of life in the Army. Of course, the only issue clothes that fit were your GI boots. This was important since infantry men spent a large portion of their time hiking - usually with a backpack.

Every Saturday the troops had to get in formation for their weekly inspection. The inspecting officer would check your rifle to see if it was spotless and if not, you would automatically get weekend duty. If your uniform didn't fit properly, that was another gig which resulted in a lecture for the first offense. A fresh haircut was required for each inspection with the length limited to 1-1/4 inches.

Since your tailor, laundry, barber and other expenses exceeded your monthly earning, you had to come up with some other source of income. I worked KP during weekends for the guys that had money coming from home. I peeled more potatoes than any other GI (also referred to as yardbird), in that Army and I have proof of that.

I recently received a package from my sister who lives near Washington, DC. It contained a letter with my old address postmarked January 1942. The letter was erroneously filed instead of being mailed and was only recently found.

It was a commendation signed by President Franklin D. Roosevelt for being the best and fastest potato peeler in the Army. A cover letter signed by President Clinton, apologizing for the undue delay of the mail was included. For all non-believers, I have both letters framed and ready for inspection.

When my funds were exhausted near the end of the month, I would be forced to take drastic measures. Since I still had some civilian clothes that I hadn't disposed of, I went to the pawn shop near the entrance to Fort Sam Houston and pawned my overcoat.

The coat was worth about $25, but I could only get $2 from the shop. Two dollars were big bucks those days, especially a week before payday. On payday I retrieved my coat.

The best thing I could do with this new-found wealth was to go to town with my buddy and sop up a few 10 cent beers. The Menger Bar, located next to the Alamo, was one of our favorite joints.

Occasionally we would go a few blocks down the street to Frenchy's Black Cat and have a couple of cold beers. Once in a while, some good-hearted soul would put a nickel in the nickelodeon and play some popular song of the 40s that would make you cry in your beer.

The area near the pawn shop was known as Snake Hill. It was a rough and rowdy place with several beer joints. The first time we explored this part of town, we witnessed a GI coming down the stairs head-first from the second story. It didn't take us long to realize that our time would be better spent in a more civilized part of town.

A buddy from my hometown of Duquesne, PA was assigned to a communications unit some distance from my outfit near the Post entrance.

His unit received orders to prepare to move to Alaska. We decided to celebrate this occasion with a farewell get-together. After a couple of beers, the bartender reminded us it was closing time.

The only thing we could buy to take out was a bottle of cheap wine. We left the tavern and headed for the River Walk where we could relax and watch the people go by. We would take a nip from the wine bottle every once in a while and reminisce about back home.

The next thing I knew, it was daylight and time to get back to camp. We had fallen asleep on he benches along the River Walk.

The other favorite place for soldiers to frequent was Breckendridge Park. It was only about a mile from our barracks, so we didn't mind the walk. There were a lot of people who visited the park on weekends and there was an abundance of young ladies.

The biggest attraction was a nickelodeon and a dance area nearby. As soon as the music started playing, the soldiers found partners to dance with and enjoyed the songs of the 40s. Jitterbugging was in vogue and most of the Yankees loved to dance.

One of the soldiers from our company was a great dancer. He could spend hours dancing during the heat of day and never get tired. The unusual thing about him was his inability to march or hike. He had the flattest feet in the Army. It was diagnosed as third degree flat feet, which meant he was unfit for combat duty.

He was transferred out of our combat unit and sent to post headquarters, which was a non-combat unit. Several months later I saw him walking the beat as an MP in the Austin area. Only the Army could make such a command decision.

In spite of all these brilliant Army rules, we were able to prepare our troops for combat and eventually face the enemy and win the war to end all wars.

CLEANLINESS MOST IMPORTANT TO ARMY DURING WWII
Sunday, August 10, 1997

There was one thing the military believed in. That was cleanliness.

As long as we were in permanent type housing, there was no excuse for not being absolutely spic and span clean. Our uniforms were always freshly cleaned and pressed. Personal hygiene was a number one priority.

I was in the infantry during the WWII era and would spend a great deal of time training in the field usually under primitive conditions. Sometimes we would be gone several days at a time from our permanent barracks.

Crawling through wooded areas in the heat of the day was part of the training. Occasionally we had night maneuvers and that was one of the things I wasn't very fond of, since we had to fight off ticks, mosquitoes, armadillos and snakes.

One night after a hard day of training, I started to crawl into my bedroll. Suddenly I felt something crawling up my leg. I came out of that bedroll like I was shot from a cannon.

I didn't sleep much that night and I didn't get back into that bedroll, either. At daybreak I inspected the bedroll and of course, there was nothing there. Whatever it was it didn't stay around till daylight.

During a night maneuver, we were given orders to prepare for a battle to conquer Neutzie Hill. We were positioned at the foot of the hill and were told to wait for further instructions. Sometime before daylight, we were given the order to charge up the hill.

As we neared the crest, a smoke screen was encountered that obscured our view. We crawled to the top of the hill through the smoke screen and engaged the enemy. We were given great reviews for our capture of the famed Neutzie Hill.

Back at our base the next day we were glad to get into the shower to clean up and treat the insect and tick bites. The only way to get the ticks out of our skin, since they bury, was to use the heat from a cigarette to have them back out. Since most of the ticks managed to get on our backs, we had to get a buddy to hold the lighted cigarette to the tick.

There was a young lad about 17 years old in our platoon. He must have been a hillbilly since he didn't know what running water was used for. His personal hygiene left much to be desired.

We got him into the shower and gave him the old GI shower. We almost wore out his skin, but we got him clean. He didn't need any more lessons after that.

We nicknamed him Tweddle-O-Twill. Any new recruits who came into our outfit were given the "Tweddle-O-Twill" treatment if they had some unclean personal habits.

After living through the field maneuvers, we were anxious to go to town and take in the sights. One of my buddies wasn't too fond of beer, so we found a place that served a good orange soda drink for 10 cents. They served peanuts with the drink at no extra charge.

We would get our fill of peanuts after a couple of sodas and then would roam the streets of San Antonio. There were several tattoo places along our route and we would stop and watch the soldiers getting tattoos. There was always a line waiting to get tattoos and we would get into line with the other GIs.

We never did get our tattoos since we would get impatient and leave before they would get to us, I'm grateful I didn't get tattooed, for I realize now how foolish I would have been to get my body permanently scarred.

About August 1941, we went on a two-month training exercise in east Texas. Some of the training was in the beautiful pine forest near the Louisiana border.

We talked to a forest ranger who happened by one day and asked him the value of the nearby land. He told us we could buy any amount for $10 an acre. The trees were about 10 years old and were well cared for.

My buddy thought it would be a good investment, but I didn't think I would ever be back in this part of the country, so I decided not to buy. My buddy was a native Texan from near San Antonio, so he decided to buy a few acres. I'm sure it was a good investment. The lumber cut from a few acres would bring a tidy sum today.

We moved out of those beautiful piney woods to another area near the Louisiana border. We got into some rugged scrub growth area infested with poison ivy. I got a good dose.

After several days, I was sent to Camp Polk for further treatment. The poison ivy infection healed in a few days and I was ready to be discharged. Since the maneuvers would last only about two more weeks, it was decided a group of us from the hospital would be sent back to Fort Sam Houston near San Antonio.

There was an old sergeant in our group who was put in charge of the 10 soldiers sent back to camp. He was a rugged looking soldier complete with red nose and ruddy complexion. You could tell he was a boozer.

The military issued meal tickets and travel tickets for the sergeant and 10 others. It was customary to do this instead of issuing individual tickets.

We were transported from the hospital to Texarkana by GI truck. It was about three hours before train time and it was near meal time. We found a nice restaurant and had supper there.

Three of us got friendly with the sergeant and decided to use some of the meal tickets to buy beer and whisky. The meal ticket were honored in any place that sold food, so we found a bar that was a very likely place.

We made a deal with the bartender and got a case of beer and a bottle of whisky. We managed to get it on the train without anyone seeing our stash. The four of us stayed up most of the night sipping our meal ticket purchase.

Next morning we all had breakfast together and all went well. Dinner time arrived and the guys wanted to go to lunch. Since we used up all the lunch tickets, we had to tell the guys they didn't issue lunch tickets.

We were scheduled to arrive at Fort Sam Houston at 4:00 p.m. that day and everyone was getting mad and hungry. I figured that someone would squeal on us and we would get into real trouble. Fortunately, we were not reported.

I promised then that I would never get involved in any more shady deals as long as I remained in the Army.

MILITARY REUNION REVIVES MEMORIES
Sunday, November 27, 1994

My wife and I attended the reunion of the 102nd Infantry Division Association held in Denver, CO August 21-27.

Anyone who served with the 102nd Infantry Division during combat in Europe from September 1944 to May 1945 is eligible to be a member of the association. We have been attending these reunions for the past 10 years and look forward to seeing our Ozark buddies and their wives each year.

The attendance of 780 was somewhat less than the average of 850 for the past few years. We have had as many as 1,000 attend past reunions. The age of our members may have something to do with the drop in attendance.

Our youngest members are at least 69 years old and the oldest are pushing 85. In order to reverse the trend of low attendance, we are going to great lengths to locate our buddies who have not become members of our association. A special coordinator program was inaugurated about five years ago to help locate our lost buddies.

I was caught in one of my weak moments and volunteered to be coordinator for Headquarters Battery, 380th Field Artillery Battalion. I later assumed the responsibility of C Battery, 380th Field Artillery Battalion. Presently I am assistant division coordinator in charge of four battalions. I don't remember how I got so deeply involved in the program.

Our objective is to get a coordinator for each unit of artillery, infantry and special troops. The duty of the coordinator is to contact every member of his unit and convince him to become a member of the 102nd Infantry Division Association.

For several years we have used the addresses from our division history book dated 1946. Unfortunately a large number of these addresses are no longer valid. About half of the letters sent out were returned because of change of address, inadequate address, no such address, or other reasons.

Some letters were sent to the proper address since they were not returned but were not answered. Still, we managed to contact former Ozarks who joined our association.

A few months ago, we hit upon a new method of contacting our buddies. We learned that compact discs for computers are available that give us up-to-date addresses and telephone numbers. They system is called CD-ROM telephone compact discs. There were two discs available, one covering the eastern half of the United States and the other covering the west.

Several of our members have computers and volunteered to use them to help locate lost buddies. We have since located several hundred men and hope to find several hundred more in the next few months with this new approach.

It's a great thrill to talk to your former comrades who you haven't seen for almost 50 years. Of course, it's always sad to talk to the widows. Many times we get word from daughters and sons and sometimes grandchildren of a veteran we have inquired about.

What a wonderful feeling it is to meet your buddies at these conventions. We have re-lived the war years at each convention and enjoyed telling stores about our experiences. Some of the stories are re-told each year, but we still enjoy them.

We rarely discuss the hardships we were through, but occasionally someone will bring out the humor of some of these events and we all have a hearty laugh. I am glad I had the opportunity to serve my country during WWII, but I wouldn't want to do it again. This was a one-time experience I will forever remember.

It all started in June 1940. I volunteered to work for the city of Duquesne, PA to assist in recording the mandatory draft of all men between the ages of 18 and 38. The world was in a turmoil with Hitler sweeping across Europe and Japan rattling her saber at us in the Pacific.

The first draft was put into action in November 1940 with only a token number of men called. Congress passed legislation that required all able-bodied men to serve their country for a minimum of 12 months. The first major draft took place in January 1941.

I was notified about a month before I was to report for induction on January 18, 1941 at the old post office in Pittsburgh. Our local draft board invited the 10 of us who were drafted to a dinner reception. The board was made up of WWI veterans and they were proud of their service.

They told some stories of their experiences during WWI and suggested various branches of service we could serve in. One of the veterans suggested the Quartermaster Corps since they had only one causality. A 100-pound bag of beans fell on his head and killed him.

We were all patriotic, as was the entire nation. I was an apprentice forger in the blacksmith shop in the steel mills in Duquesne when I was drafted. My foreman told me he could get me a deferment for a year, but I told him I wanted to serve.

I reported for induction on the appointed date and spent most of the day going through various physical exams. I felt I could pass all the exams except my eye test.

As we stood in line for the eye test, I managed to see the chart while awaiting my turn. I memorized most of the chart because I knew I couldn't see more than the top letter with my right eye. I barely passed the test because I didn't memorize enough to pass with flying colors.

The eye doctor thought I partied too much the night before. I finally got his okay and went on to the next exam breathing a sigh of relief. I didn't feel I could face my family or friends if I failed. I didn't want to be classified unfit for military service.

All the men who passed their physicals were called to be sworn in at 4:00 p.m. the same day. It was a great feeling. I was bubbling with pride. We were advised that we would be boarding the train that night and were going to Fort Meade, MD for formal induction. I called my folks.

After receiving our uniforms, we were on our way to the 2nd Infantry Division at Fort Sam Houston in San Antonio.

Because of the deteriorating world condition, Congress passed legislation to extend our enlistment to 18 months effective June 1941. Then the bombing of Pearl Harbor by the Japanese on December 7, 1941 caused our duty to be extended indefinitely.

In August 1942, I was sent to Camp Maxey in Paris, TX to help organize the 102nd Infantry Division. We went overseas in September 1944 and fought the Germans from the Siegfried Line at the Holland-German border to within 40 miles of Berlin at the Elbe River.

My one-year military draft duty ended after five years and four months and I am just as proud and patriotic today as I was when I was drafted in January 1941.

There's a Lighter Side To Guard Duty
Sunday, July 21, 1996

Guard duty in the military was one duty that you could not shirk or trade off with your buddies. I was assigned duty to patrol the officer's family quarters at Fort Sam Houston, TX. My duty hours were from 11:00 p.m. to 7:00 a.m. I had to walk the area in the alley behind the officer's homes and check in every two hours with the sergeant of the guard.

The phones were located in about the middle of the alleys. I had enough leisure time to drop in at the Officer's Club in the area to have coffee until closing time. The club usually stayed open until about 1:00 a.m.

After the club closed, I had about an hour of spare time after I made each round in the area. It was summertime and I enjoyed the night air and would find a place to sit down and marvel at the stars in the heavens.

About 3:00 a.m. one morning, I got sleepy after doing duty all day the previous day before my night shift began. I found an open garage that had a nice looking car that I decided to check out.

I sat down and planned to rest for a short while. A terrible thing happened. I fell asleep and was awakened by the bright sun shining in my face. It was about 6:30 a.m. and sleeping in an officer's car while on guard duty is a very stupid thing to do.

I dashed to the nearest phone and reported in to the sergeant of the guard. Fortunately he was half asleep and didn't miss my calls that I failed to make. If caught, I could have been court-martialed and thrown into the brig. My guardian angel saved me from another tragedy.

After a few months of infantry training we were told that we would be given military police training. I enjoyed the 10-12 mile daily hikes and other infantry duties and wasn't too interested in military police training.

Our military police training involved all sorts of specialized skills. We spent several hours tumbling outdoors using mattresses to help break our falls. After we got the knack of doing this, it became a fun thing for us. I looked forward to this daily exercise that lasted several weeks.

For additional training we were paired up with someone about our size to box with. We used oversized gloves for training purposes so that our nose and teeth would not require extensive cosmetic surgery during the training period.

A captain who was an expert in jujitsu was called in to teach us this ancient art. For some reasons he picked me to practice the various holds and he flipped me into the air and onto my back several times. We were glad this training was over because it could be hazardous to our health. Of course, we were being trained to make this hazardous to the health of others who were not abiding by the laws of order.

Our company was scheduled to have bayonet training about this time, even though it had nothing to do with our military police training. A sergeant by the name of Bronkhurst was in charge of this training. He was the personal representative of Gen. Kreuger, who was commander of all troops in the Eighth Service Command.

This sergeant was tough as nails and he could bark loud enough to be heard two blocks away. We were required to fix bayonets and stab the enemy (bales of hay in the form of a man) in the chest. If the bayonet didn't go through the entire bale of hay, you were not going to survive in actual combat, according to the military experts.

After several weeks of training we were placed on MP duty. This duty was to last only two months, since the regular MPs were on maneuvers and they were to take over as soon as they returned.

My first assignment was to ride the bus from Fort Sam Houston to downtown San Antonio on payday weekend. This duty started at 5:00 p.m. and lasted until midnight.

The bus route would take us through downtown and on to the far end of town. There were quite a few honky tonks along the route and the soldiers would get off and on at their favorite beer joints. I was required to stand at the doorway next to the bus driver and keep order on the bus. I had a good size billy club and a .45 pistol to help keep the soldiers in line. The MP arm band was also a deterrent.

I never did have any serious problems with the GIs, since the MP arm band and billy club seemed to have a soothing effect on the soldiers as they entered the bus. Even the obnoxious drunk soldiers knew that they didn't want to be sobered up with a fractured skull caused by an innocent looking billy club.

The last stop was usually the 23rd Infantry Regiment. As the soldiers unloaded, I would always stop the last four and have them carry out the GIs who had passed out. They would be laid out on the lawn to sober up, which usually would happen about daylight. After a good cold shower in the morning, they would be ready for duty.

These military experiences helped me accept the challenges of life these many years since WWII.

MILITARY REUNION LIKE FAMILY GATHERING
Sunday, August 18, 1996

I attended the 102nd Infantry Division Reunion in Louisville and enjoyed visiting with my WWII buddies again. The 1996 reunion was one of the best I have attended the past few years. I have often dreamed of going to the historic Churchill Downs and I'm glad I finally got a chance to go.

The reunion committee did a great job of arranging for the interesting tours. We arrived Tuesday afternoon via American Airlines from Dallas-Fort Worth International Airport. We missed out on the distillery tour scheduled for Tuesday. They no longer give samples of their product and it's probably a good thing. We have some very hardy drinkers in our group.

Wednesday morning about 10 bus loads of our comrades and wives headed for Churchill Downs. We have all watched the Kentucky Derby on TV at least once and we know it's one of the most fabulous and colorful events seen on the tube. We had a guided tour of the famous track and a movie of some of the highlights of great races of yesteryear.

Our entire group was seated on Millionaire's Row and was served a fine buffet lunch. We were on the fourth level near the finish line of this beautiful and historic Churchill Downs. Mint juleps, the drink of the rich and famous, were served by our very efficient waitresses. We were instructed to chew a bit of the mint to give a refreshing taste to the palate. I had one drink and enjoyed it. If you wish to imbibe another mint julep, you probably couldn't care less if your palate is refreshed or not.

The races began shortly after lunch and we all decided to invest a few bucks. Pat Day, the famous jockey who used to race at Hot Springs, was on the program for the first five races. I bet on him the first four races and would you believe, he got lost in the shuffle in all four. He won the Kentucky Derby but couldn't win a small time race for me. He won the fifth race, but I lost faith in him and didn't bet on that one.

On Thursday we took the tour to Fort Knox and the Patton Museum. A memorial service was held at the Post Theater with approximately 400 in attendance. We were served lunch in the non-commissioned Officers Club with GIs helping the civilian staff service our hungry group.

Our next major event was lunch and cruise on the *Star of Louisville* on the beautiful Ohio River. (Of course, it was muddy from all the recent rain.) Pictures were made by a professional photographer as we boarded our ship.

After the cruise, the pictures were ready for previewing. We were impressed with our picture and bought two to be placed in our family album. We enjoyed our lunch and comradeship during the two-hour cruise.

Saturday night was banquet night, with everyone dressed in their best bib and tucker. A memorial service was held with a candle being lit for each combat unit of the 102nd Infantry Division. All members would rise as their unit was announced. It was a solemn occasion with *Taps* being played to honor all those who gave their lives for their country.

The banquet dinner was superb, with about 800 in attendance. The waiters and waitresses were efficient and courteous and served the entire group in about a half hour.

The hospitality room was open every afternoon and evening. It was great to relax and visit with comrades we look forward to seeing each reunion. It is like a large family reunion with a lot of hugging and embracing. One develops a lot of close ties with many of his comrades and their wives by attending these annual reunions.

We were entertained each evening by various musical groups in the hospitality room. The beautiful songs of the 40s were enjoyed by all. One group was composed of various sized harmonicas that produced a beautiful sound. Another group was a four-piece band that sounded like some of the big bands of the 30s. Some of the more agile types danced the evening away.

We are looking forward to our next reunion in San Francisco in 1997 and San Antonio in 1998.

PEARL HARBOR BOMBING HAS IMMEDIATE IMPACT AT ARMY CAMP
Sunday, December 7, 1997

I was stationed at Fort Sam Houston, San Antonio on December 7, 1941.

I was drafted January 18 of that year to serve my country for one year. Because of the tense world situation, the one year was extended 18 months in July of 1941 and after Pearl Harbor, it was for the duration.

I seldom went to town, except on weekends, if I wasn't working KP for some of my more affluent buddies who were getting money from home. The $21 per month pay that was increased to $30 wasn't enough to take care of the essential. Uncle Sam didn't furnish everything for his soldiers. The laundry, tailor, barber and other miscellaneous expenses were the soldier's responsibility.

I enjoyed going to town on Sunday afternoon with a buddy just to get away from the Army routine. Sunday, December 7, 1941 was a typical mild day with temperatures in the 70s. My buddy and I would walk to the downtown area and just take in the sights. We went to our favorite spot to get a refreshing orange drink for 10 cents. Peanuts were served with the drink at no extra cost and we ate all we wanted.

While enjoying our drink, a news flash came over the radio: "All soldiers from the 2nd Infantry Division, return to your units immediately." We left for the bus stop and returned to camp.

On the way back we heard rumors of the Japanese bombing Pearl Harbor and that their ships were sighted off the California coast. The anti-aircraft guns were already being placed in strategic locations on the post under camouflaged cover.

We reported into our company headquarters and were told to get into our combat fatigues and wait for further orders. Later on that night we got orders to turn in certain items and prepare to leave at a moment's notice. We didn't get much sleep that night and were glad to see the sun come up the next morning.

We were on standby for several hours on the morning of December 8. We got word that President Roosevelt made a speech on the radio and declared war against the Japanese. We got official word that Pearl Harbor was bombed and that we lost almost all of

Class A Uniform, 2nd Division, 1941, Fort Sam Houston.

our Navy that was stationed there. Our West Coast was feared threatened and several military units were sent to patrol there.

Our division was to be prepared to leave on short notice but were to continue our training until further notice. All the Japanese were being rounded up and sent to camps that were being prepared by the military to keep them under the watchful eye of our military forces.

Patriotism was at an all-time high. Radical organizations were being kept under surveillance by the FBI and other government agencies. An unpatriotic comment would land someone in confinement for an indefinite period.

This was the first time our country was ever threatened by a foreign power since the American Revolution. The government and all our industries geared for the greatest military buildup in the history of the US. Several million people were involved in military operations throughout the world.

Our enemies miscalculated the will of our people. Everyone made sacrifices, including the women and children on the homefront. Never again will we be unprepared. God Bless America.

After being transferred to help organize another infantry division, we finally went overseas and got into combat on the Holland-

German border. This is where the Germans had their permanent fortifications known as the Siegfried Line. This is where the most brutal battles were fought.

The rest is history and I am thankful that I survived and made it back home to my family.

WAR LEADS TO LATE CELEBRATION
Sunday, December 21, 1997

It was November 10, 1945 when I received word that I would be on my way home in a few days.

We were doing occupation duties in Germany after the war and we were all waiting for our turn to leave for the good old USA. I had accumulated 95 points, a system based on years of service, overseas duty and other criteria.

There were several men from our 102nd Infantry Division who also were qualified. It was a great day when we bid farewell to our buddies. We traveled by GI truck to the nearest train station, then on to our destination to Cherbourg, which was our point of embarkation. The antique train we rode was used to carry 40 men or eight horses. Such trains were generally known as *40 & 8s.*

We arrived at Lucky Strike Camp, which was one of the holding areas in Cherbourg. It happened to be a bald desert prairie as flat as the salt flats of Utah. The wind would blow in from the ocean and the clouds of dust would fill the air. This was to be our home until our ship arrived.

We lived in two-man tents with very little comforts of home. We had a pot belly stove that was to supply the heat to keep us from freezing in the 30 degree temperatures. Because of the ration of six ounces of wood per man per day, everyone managed to spend time at the PX (post exchange). Most of us had limited duties, so card playing was about the only activity to pass away the time.

When I got ready to go to bed, I would fire up the stove with my allotment of wood to thaw out the covers on the cot. One night after crawling into my bed with the fire blazing, I got a call to report to personnel headquarters immediately. I jumped into my clothes and off I went.

After the problems were resolved, I started back to my tent. As I neared the area, I saw a tent in full blaze with fire trucks rushing to the scene. I suddenly realized it was my tent.

My tent buddy, Capt. Smith had arrived in time to salvage some of our belongings. He braved the smoke and fire and threw out our footlockers and some of our other possessions.

We were fortunate we were not asleep in the tent with that raging fire. We had ammunition and pistols that could have blown us to kingdom come. I lost my uniforms in the fire and had to make arrangements to go to Paris the next morning to purchase uniforms for the trip home. The Army had a PX in Paris that had a good supply of uniforms and other soldier essentials.

I was furnished a Jeep and driver for the trip to Paris, which was about 60 miles from our camp. It started to snow as we prepared to leave for the big city. I instructed my driver to be careful on these treacherous roads because I didn't want to wind up in hospital and miss my trip home.

He assured me that he would be careful since he was looking forward to going home also. He had sent his mother more than $20,000 he had won gambling and he wanted to enjoy spending it on things he had dreamed about for a long time. We made the trip to Paris and back without problems.

After several weeks at Camp Lucky Strike, we got orders to travel to southern France. None of the boats were due to arrive in Cherbourg, but a boat was due to dock at a port in southern France in the near future.

We boarded the infamous *40 & 8s* again for the trip to southern France. We had a pot bellied stove in our car. It was bitter cold and we fired up the old stove to get warm. Our trip lasted about two days since we had to be sidetracked several times to let other trains pass.

We finally arrived at our destination in southern France and stayed two days to get everything in order to board our ship. We were told what items we could take back to the States which included one pistol each that most of us had requisitioned from German POWs.

A Victory ship finally arrived and off we sailed on December 20, 1945. The Victory ship was designed to haul freight, which was loaded in the hold of the ship. On this trip there would be no freight except our footlockers, which didn't take up much space. The boat ride was fairly smooth until about the fifth day, when we ran into a storm in the middle of the Atlantic.

Our ship had a salty old captain who had been through many storms in his life. Several of us were on deck when the storm hit without warning. We were ordered below and lashed down the hatches.

The captain changed course to miss some of the storm, but we were battered for four days. We were on the high seas for Christmas, fighting for survival. We thought the old Victory ship would break apart in the storm.

We finally reached Fort Patrick Henry in Virginia on New Year's Day. After several hours of trying, I finally got a call through to my wife in Paris, TX. She promised to keep up the Christmas tree until I got home.

After several more days of delay getting the paperwork done, I received my discharge and arrived home January 10, 1946. I celebrated Christmas with my wife and daughter, thanking God I made it back for Christmas, even though I was few days late.

LEARNING THE TERRIBLE TRUTH ABOUT WAR
Sunday, August 30, 1998

After many months of training stateside we were declared ready for combat in Europe during WWII. We arrived at Fort Dix located near the east coast in late July 1944 to prepare for shipment overseas. After several weeks of specialized training we were sent to Camp Kilmer for final last minute instructions regarding our trip overseas.

We left Camp Kilmer after three days of final preparation and arrived at the East River to take the ferry to our boat in the New York Harbor. Everything was top secret as far as our trip was concerned and we rode the ferry under blackout conditions. When we arrived at the pier where our boat was located, a military band greeted us with a typical military march that made your hair stand on edge. Of course our departure was top secret but our troops were the only ones observing this secrecy. I never could understand some of these military policies.

It took several hours to load the troops on our ship since each person's name had to be called out as he approached the gang plank. At this time we were given instructions to where we were to be housed. Every soldier was also given a meal card which was color coded so he could know the time he was to be fed.

The boat was designed to accommodate about 500 first class passengers but since it was being used to haul military personnel the total was increased to 5,000 troops. Feeding of troops required three one-hour shifts to accommodate all the personnel. The color coded cards indicated the time you were to line up to eat. There were one hour intervals for each card and if you didn't get in line at the right time you just missed your meal.

Breakfast and supper were typical meals but lunch was soup and crackers or coffee and cookies. There were no seats at the dining areas because of space limitations. There were make-shift narrow tables that were used for standing room only eating. Chow lines began at 5:00 a.m. and lasted practically all day to about 7:00 p.m. Many of the GIs would rather spend their time shooting dice than standing in line to eat. Some enjoyed reading "Pocket Books" to pass the time.

Our boat was so crowded that it was almost impossible to get from one end of the boat to the other end. The decks were so crowded that in case of an emergency you would die before you could get to the first aid station. There were just enough lifeboats to take most of the ship's crew if they could reach the lifeboat. Our boat left the New York Harbor about daylight and we got into a convoy formation with Navy protection in front and on our flanks. Our entire division of 15,000 men and several other units were in this convoy.

About mid-afternoon the first day out of the harbor German submarines were sighted. Depth charges were dropped on our flanks by our Navy which was to protect us from these submarines.

The Germans had their spies all along the east coast and they knew every move that was being made by our military.

About 9:00 p.m. the first night out an alarm was sounded for all troops to prepare for an emergency. We grabbed our life jackets and were advised to standby. If we had any atheists in our midst they became converts in a hurry. Fear will make men do strange things. We got the all clear report an hour later and we breathed a sigh of relief. I didn't sleep much that night and I didn't sleep much the rest of the 12-day trip across the Atlantic Ocean.

Hammock type bunks were the sleeping accommodations for most of the GIs. These sleeping quarters were in the "hold" of the ship and it was very hot and lacked air conditioning. Many of the GIs got seasick and there was nothing that could be done medically to give them some relief. Most of the GIs went up on deck and stayed there during the entire trip.

I stayed on the deck of the ship most of the time except during chow time. We watched the sea gulls dive into the ocean to catch their daily ration of fish. Sea gulls were a hardy breed that could ride the waves for hours at a time. There were schools of porpoises that followed our ship across the ocean. They were fun to watch as they frolicked in the ocean a few feet behind our boat. They lived off the fish they could catch and they also enjoyed the food in the trash that was dumped into the ocean each night.

We had pleasant weather during our 12 days on the ocean and it felt good to be on deck breathing the cool salt air. The constant up and down movement of the boat made our stomach rumble and made you feel quite uncomfortable at times. At night the convoy would change course several times to make it difficult for the German submarines to keep track of us. We were very grateful for the Navy for protecting us during our entire trip across the ocean.

We finally arrived at a port in southern England where we spent the night. The next morning we crossed the English Channel single file without Navy protection. The waters in the channel were very rough and we took a real beating for about three hours until we dropped anchor in the harbor at Cherbourg, France. We were transferred to a ferry for the short trip to the shore.

After a couple hours of waiting with full field packs weighing about 50 pounds we were finally brought to shore by our ferry. We were loaded on GI trucks about dark to our bivouac area to spend the night. All this was done under blackout conditions. We were told the mines were cleared to the edge of the road and reminded not to leave our bivouac area. We set up our pup tents in the rain and was glad to unload our backpacks that had made our back and shoulders numb from the heavy load.

After two days in this area where the initial battles were fought in the hedgerows we were assigned duties to haul supplies from the ships to Paris for our troops who were engaged in combat just outside Paris and other areas in northern France.

About 30 days later we were sent to the Holland-German border to engage the enemy near the permanent fortifications of the famed Siegfried Line. There we learned how terrible war can be as the causalities started to be brought back to the rear areas. We all wondered if we would be the next casualty or if we would live yet to see another day.

"BED CHECK CHARLIE" KEPT TROOPS ALERT IN THEIR WWII FOXHOLES
Sunday, November 8, 1998

There are numerous memories that last a lifetime from service during WWII in Europe. At night we usually stayed in basements of bombed out buildings, underground makeshift shelters, improvised caves or foxholes. The Germans were sending V-2 rockets to England each evening and we could hear them as they passed over our area. If we were brave enough to come out of our hideouts, we could see the rockets which looked like a big cigar with the red glow of the tail end.

The rockets devastated the London area for two or three years until our Air Force came to the rescue. Our Air Force, together with the Royal Air Force, made numerous bombing runs to knock out the German installations where the V-2 rockets were assembled. Another trick that our pilots learned was to get close enough to tip the wings of the rockets to throw them off course so they would explode harmlessly over the English Channel.

Bed Check Charlie, a lone German fighter plane, would usually make his rounds each evening to remind us that it wasn't safe to get out of our hideouts if we planned to be around for another day.

Berlin Annie was another one of our evening visitors by radio. Some of the guys managed to have battery operated radios to pick up her evening programs. She would play some of the most sentimental tunes of the 40s to make you feel homesick. She would tell us that our girlfriends and wives back home were having a big time while we were risking our lives fighting in Germany. She would tell us that England was not doing their share and that we were fools for fighting their war. She did everything she could to break down the morale of our troops.

The Germans also dropped propaganda leaflets on our troops. These were similar to statements made by Berlin Annie. They would also have pictures of girls back home having good times with guys who escaped the draft. They made every effort to make us homesick.

The constant bombing by our Air Force played havoc with the industries in all the larger cities in Germany. Food was getting very scarce and people were hard-pressed to get enough food to survive. The military had priority over everything.

Our planes flying from England to their targets in Germany would carry auxiliary gas tanks for the required fuel for the round trip back to England. They would release the empty tanks all over the countryside as the fuel was used up. These tanks usually contained a quart or so of fuel which was a very scarce item for the local folks who lived in the areas where the tanks would be dropped. The German government warned the people that these tanks were probably booby trapped and should not be touched. It didn't take long for the local folks to realize that there was no danger in retrieving the tanks and using the previous fuel for their own needs.

The Nazi government knew the allies were winning the war and continued to tell folks how well things were going. In order to boost their morale, they would run trains with signs on the boxcars that said that it was another load of secret weapons being sent to the front to destroy the enemy. Hitler was really desperate when he realized that his days were numbered. They kept up the propaganda until the bitter end.

We used Dutch soldiers to guard our installations in the rear areas so that our regular troops could be used for more important missions. Most of these soldiers were young men about 17-19 years of age. At night they were told to ask for the password before they would let anyone approach these installations. These guards would hide in the dark shadows so they could not be seen. They couldn't speak English so when they hollered "Halt," you better halt.

On several occasions I would be returning from a trip to battalion headquarters during the hours of darkness and didn't have the new password for that night and would give the old password. They guards wouldn't let me in until their supervisor, a lieutenant, would give them the okay. It usually took several minutes before word got to their officer in charge and I never knew if these young soldiers would get nervous and decide to shoot.

Traveling at night was always hazardous since we had to travel under blackout conditions. It was almost impossible to see the road or trails that were used unless there was a full moon. You never knew when the enemy would fire a few rounds of artillery shell into our area during the hours of darkness. The Germans had all the crossroads zeroed in and it was always hazardous to approach these areas day or night. We would wait until a few rounds were fired and then go like hell through these crossroads before the next rounds were fired. We considered ourselves lucky each time we made it without being hit. We often wondered how long our luck would hold out.

True Spirit Found In Bombed Out Basement
Sunday, December 13, 1998

We were temporarily located in the city of Herleen, Holland about the first week of November 1944. Our kitchen was setup on one of the streets in this city that was on the Holland-German border.

After the troops were fed the leftover food was given to the children who were lined up holding small containers to take the food home to their families. We were housed in vacant homes and other buildings in this Dutch border town.

Our infantry was placed in service with other seasoned troops to get their first battle experience. A few days later our artillery was placed into service to support the infantry in the battle to breach the famed Siegfried Line.

The Germans had permanent fortifications made of concrete and steel eight to 10 feet thick. In addition to these pill boxes there were numerous other obstacles consisting of tank traps, concrete emplacements and numerous minefields. This is what we had to look forward to for the next several months.

Our stay at Herleen lasted only a few days but we made many friends with the children and parents of the wonderful Dutch city. They were glad to see us since they no longer had to put up with the Germans who occupied their country for a longtime.

By the end of November we were moved to Palenberg, a bombed out German village with only a few damaged homes left standing. A part of a damaged coal mine Administration Building was to be our headquarters for the seeable future.

As we were unloading our equipment a lone German plane swooped down and strafed our entire area with .50 caliber bullets. You could see the dust fly as the bullets hit the ground. Through some miracle not one of our men were hit and we were very thankful for that.

We had telephone communications with our battalion headquarters and we would get messages daily from the battalion commander or his staff. When the telephone lines were cut messengers were used to get the information delivered.

I usually had to make trips to battalion headquarters every few days. Many times the roads were almost impassable with mud up to the hubcaps of our jeep. We used aerial photos to find our way since there were few permanent type roads to many of these areas. Usually we followed telephone lines that were strung along the makeshift roads to locate our battalion headquarters.

On many occasions enemy artillery would be encountered and we would floorboard the gas and try to outrun the shrapnel. We prayed that our luck would hold out one more time. We would always make an effort to get our business done at battalion headquarters before it got dark.

Traveling at night during blackout conditions was very hazardous. What a relief it was to get back to our outfit without being hit by enemy fire or by friendly troop fire.

One of the duties I had was to visit all our battalion gun positions and take care of the personal needs of the troops. It took me several days to make the rounds crawling in and out of the camouflaged gun positions. Many of the guys had money they wanted to send home to their folks and I took care of all these and other personal problems. I had a time keeping track of all the different types of currency, which included invasion currency, French francs, German marks and Dutch currency.

A bitter winter arrived with plenty of snow to add to the problems our troops were faced with but it was better than the knee-deep mud. We took advantage of the fresh fallen snow and made snow ice cream by using our powered lemon to flavor the snow. It wasn't a gourmet treat but it was a good substitute for dessert, which we didn't get with our C or K-rations. It was a welcome change from the Kangaroo Stew (C-Ration Stew) that we had so very often.

There was a lull in the fighting for a few days about the first week of December. We got word that a movie *Rhapsody in Blue* would be shown in a bombed out theater and we could send a few of our section to see it. I managed to get on the list and we had to walk about two miles cross-country in the snow to the theater.

The windows were all knocked out and there was no heat in the building. We got through three hours of this wonderful movie shivering from the bitter cold. As we were leaving one of the Dutch guards, a young teenager accidentally fired a few rounds from his automatic rifle that barely missed us. Our guardian angel saved us from another tragic incident.

Christmas time was nearing and thoughts of home were on our minds. Some of the boys found small bushes that they used to decorate for Christmas. Paper wrapping from home and other miscellaneous items were used on the make believe Christmas trees.

I managed to give each one of my section a gift. I used items sent from home, which included Christmas cards, old keys, cigarette lighters and other miscellaneous items, which they seemed to appreciate very much. It was the thought that really spread the spirit of Christmas.

One of the best presents we all had was a trip back to Herleen, Holland to take a shower where the coal mines had bathing facilities to handle a large number of troops. It was times like these that we learn to appreciate the basic needs of survival and give thanks for all that we have.

The true spirit of Christmas was found in a bombed out basement.

ALL WERE NOT HEROES DURING COMBAT OF WWII
Sunday, May 30, 1999

It was December 16, 1944 and our location was a few miles inside of Germany from the Holland border. It was a typical winter day with temperatures near freezing, but fog had rolled in overnight and visibility was down to just a few feet.

Our 102nd Infantry Division was in the midst of planning the offensive across the Roer River. We had two tank divisions and an infantry division in our area and that was to be part of the drive across the Roer River.

Things started happening during the days that seemed very unusual. A lot of troop movement was going on that was not planned in our area of operation. The tank divisions and infantry division were moving out and we wondered what was taking our place. Our division was ordered to protect the entire front where these troops had been in place. No one seemed to know what was going on.

A day or so later we were told that the Germans were advancing with a massive number of tanks, infantry troops and artillery about 50 miles south of our position. Hitler was determined to drive through the Allied lines and eventually push our troops into the sea. Only a mad man would take such a risk that eventually turned out to be one of the biggest military blunders Hitler made.

The Allies were caught off guard and we suffered numerous casualties. We couldn't get air support because of the dense fog. Our troops were practically encircled by the Germans and all available troops were sent into the area to drive the Germans back. Our paratroopers were dropped into the area to help relieve our troops.

The situation was critical for several days, but eventually our troops drove back the Germans. The Germans suffered numerous casualties. Many of our troops were taken prisoner. This was the beginning of the end of the German empire.

The Allies had penetrated the permanent fortifications of the Siegfried Line. The advance of our armies had been measured in yards during these battles. From now on it would be the natural barriers such as the Roer River and Rhine River to cross.

Most of the towns that were captured were small villages and farm houses that required door-to-door fighting. There were no civilians to be found as our armies moved forward. They fled before our troops got to these villages.

It was not uncommon to find food on the tables of these captured homes. The civilians had to leave in a hurry when the Germans retreated.

Prior to our offensive to the Roer River, our supplies had to be replenished. Ammunition, gasoline, tanks, artillery, food and other supplies were to be stockpiled. The enemy forces had to be determined.

Patrols were sent out at night to locate the front lines of the enemy. Prisoners had to be captured and brought back by these patrols to be interrogated by our military intelligence people. The infantry had to be prepared for a counter-offensive. Our forward observers would relay information of the enemy positions so that our artillery could fire at the various military targets.

All of our various unit command posts had to be protected day and night. Guards were stationed at these locations 24 hours a day. We had some very young replacements in our division. We needed these replacements to take the place of the causalities from battle wounds and various other ailments. Frost bite and dysentery took a heavy toll.

Some of these replacements had just arrived from the States by plane. Most of them had about four weeks training without ever seeing a gun. The first thing we had to do was take these raw recruits out to the nearest slag pile to fire a carbine and a .45 pistol.

We used these replacements to help with the guard duty at our battalion headquarters fire direction center located in a basement of a bombed-out building. One of our guards was fired upon while on guard duty. The bullet hit his canteen and grazed his helmet without doing any serious damage. This concerned everyone at the battalion headquarters and additional guards were posted.

A couple of nights later, while on guard duty, this same guard was hit again. This time the bullet went through the top of his helmet, missing his scalp by a fraction of an inch. By this time everyone was getting suspicious of these close encounters. This guard was questioned and you could tell he wasn't frightened by his experience. He wasn't telling the truth.

The military ballistic experts in Paris were notified and all the affected items were sent to Paris for testing. The results were as expected. The shots fired at the guard were from very close range - no more than two inches away.

The guard was sent to our military headquarters in Paris to face a military court martial. We did not get any information regarding the outcome of the court martial. The war continued several months and there were more important duties to perform which kept us from following up on the outcome.

Some 55 years have passed and I can't remember the name of this solider. I'm sure his parents were shocked to receive word regarding their son. This teenager was football hero in high school and in the Army he was just another GI. Maybe that's why he tried to be a hero.

BITTER WINTER TAKES TOLL ON TROOPS IN '44
Sunday, July 25, 1999

The bitter winter and record snow during the month of December 1944 took its toll on our troops of the 102nd Infantry Division.

The Battle of the Bulge near the Belgium border was finally coming to its disastrous end for the German armies. They were pushed back to their original position in the Siegfried Line that was composed of permanent concrete and steel reinforcements at critical locations.

During the battle it was reported that the Germans were dropping parachutists behind our lines to capture prisoners to be interrogated for intelligence purposes. Hitler was making his final efforts to do something to help boost the morale of his troops. He knew that the end was rapidly approaching.

I was returning from a meeting with my battalion commander during the time of the parachutist scare. We were driving under blackout conditions and the night was as black as it gets without a full moon. Guards were stationed at crossroads and other critical locations to intercept any Germans that might have parachuted into our area.

We were stopped by a guard at a crossroad. We heard someone holler HALT! We stopped immediately although we never did see the guard in the blackness of the night.

"What is your name? What outfit are you from? What is your home state? What is your hometown? What is the capital of your state?" If you couldn't answer these questions promptly you were in serious trouble, "like being shot."

Well, we answered all the questions and were given the order to proceed. We continued our journey and eventually got back to our outfit without anymore serious problems.

Our division was preparing for the battle to the Roer River. This would be the final massive assault through the Siegfried Line. All three infantry regiments were given specify military targets to capture.

The infantry companies were given snowsuits so they would blend in with the snow that had fallen the past few days. All assault activities were coordinated with the entire division and the artillery units fired thousands of rounds of ammunition at the enemy fortifications. This was the most devastating infantry and artillery firepower that was used against the Germans by the 102nd Infantry Division.

After the battle to the Roer was over, we learned that some of the Siegfried Line fortifications were abandoned because of the intense and massive infantry and artillery firepower demoralized some of the German defenders. This was a great victory for our troops.

Plans were being finalized to prepare for the crossing of the Roer River. Our unit was moving into the town of Linnich to stay there until the crossing was made. We were greeted by a lone German plane that strafed us as we lined up for chow. The .50 caliber bullets peppered our entire area without causing a single casualty. Miracles like these are why some of us are still around to talk about it.

It was about the middle of February 1944 when the Roer River crossing was planned. Normally the river was just a few feet wide. The water upstream was controlled by a dam. The gates were opened and the Roer River became a treacherous river with a swift current.

The narrow river suddenly became a massive body of water about a mile wide in places. Small boats were used for the initial crossing. Our infantry suffered considerable casualties during the crossing. By the end of February 1944 most of our division units had made the crossing.

It was now time to prepare for the battle north to the city of Krefeld, which was located about 50 miles north. Supplies of gasoline, ammunition, food, clothing and another military items had to be trucked to all of our division units.

There were few permanent fortifications left, but the Germans didn't want to give up this part of their homeland without defending each village regardless of casualties. Up until now there were very few civilians to be found since they fled as their armies retreated.

The advance of our troops was slowed down by the series of canals and other military obstacles that were encountered. There were battles being fought from door to door in many of the villages. The Germans had used civilians, men, women and children to dig trenches and build other fortifications to slow down the advance of our troops.

Many of the towns that were captured had civilians that didn't have an opportunity to escape. The ones that did escape left everything they owned behind. Utilities were still available in some of the villages that were captured.

After several weeks of combat and numerous individual battles our troops finally made it into Krefeld. Streetcars were left on their tracks since everyone had to flee from the advancing armies. One of the infantry companies boarded a streetcar and rode it into town with GIs hanging on and enjoying the victory ride.

The German army retreated across the Rhine River where they planned to setup defenses to stall the advance of the Allied Armies.

There were thousands of civilians that remained in Krefeld and surrounding areas. Most of them were grateful that their part of the war was over. We were no longer the enemy and we were welcomed by most of the civilians.

Krefeld was known to be a famous spa by the German people. Our military government officers made arrangements with the local authorities to have the spa available for use by our troops. A couple of buddies and I decided to go to the spa to take the hot baths. I had a cold and I felt that the healing waters were what I need.

I introduced myself to the caretaker who was in charge of the facility. He was an elderly gentleman about five feet one inch tall. He couldn't speak English but we managed to understand each other. He placed me in a booth with numerous heat lamps mounted around the entire inside of the cubicle.

After several minutes of this treatment I was ready to get out and get into the warm mineral water that would cure all my ailments. I was getting extremely hot and needed to get out of the steam bath, but the caretaker was nowhere to be found.

After sometime, it seemed like hours, my little German friend showed up and got me out of the hot booth and into the warm tub of mineral water. For a moment I thought he suddenly became my enemy and had plans to get even with me for all the destruction done to his homeland. Thank God he was a grateful friend that was glad that we were there to liberate his people.

WELL DESERVED REST PRECEDES OBSTACLE OF RHINE CROSSING
Sunday, September 5, 1999

About the first week of March 1945 all effective resistance inside Krefeld was withdrawn. It was now time for a much deserved rest for all the troops of the 102nd Infantry Division.

The next major offensive, crossing the Rhine River, would require several weeks of preparation. Maintenance of vehicles, tanks, guns and other military equipment would be carried out during the next few weeks.

Some of the troops would be required to secure the west bank of the Rhine River. The three to five miles from Krefeld to the river was subject to infiltration by the Germans.

The Germans retreated across the Rhine in a hurry and left many of the NAZI memorabilia behind. One of their headquarters was found which contained pictures of Hitler and his staff and numerous pictures of the German troops in parade with all their modern weapons of destruction. I managed to get some of these pictures but they got lost sometime later during our many movements to the Elbe River.

We found a post office that was vacated in a hurry by their employees leaving money in their cash registers. Packages of mail were stacked in piles ready to be sorted and mailed to their destination.

We managed to get a handful of German currency, which we thought would be useless since the country would be bankrupt by the end of the war. We kept some for souvenirs and used some after the war for bartering purposes. We attacked the piles of mail with fixed bayonets to see if there was anything of value to be found.

To the victor belongs the spoils, but the military did not approve of this idea. We probably would have been court-martialed if we were caught looting and destroying civilian goods and property.

An infantry captain was relieved of his command for participating in the streetcar victory ride into downtown Krefeld (he drove the streetcar.) The charge was conduct unbecoming an officer and a gentleman.

During the temporary lull in hostilities some of the infantry managed to board the boats that were docked along the Rhine River. The Germans had to leave the boats in a hurry during their retreat and left plenty of liquor and other items for our troops to discover.

The prize loot found were gallon jugs of Three Star Hennesy Cognac. Many of the GIs in the infantry managed to get a jug for their personal use to share with their buddies. All the booze, wine and cognac was stolen from the French during the German occupation. Our troops enjoyed this gift from the French people even though we had to steal it from the German military.

Some of the GIs were fortunate enough to get a leave of absence to visit Paris. The trip consisted of about four hours of riding in the back end of a two-ton truck to Belgium and then a several hour ride on a train to Paris.

The military had a hotel that was used to house these GIs during their stay in Paris. Meals were also served without cost at this hotel. This was military chow that was cooked and served by French cooks and waiters who were paid by our military.

Cigarettes were used to bribe the waiters to get a second helping of food. One or two cigarettes was all it took to get the additional food. A concert orchestra played dinner music for the evening meal.

Back at Krefeld, plans were being made for the crossing of the Rhine River. Patrols were crossing the river at night on three-man boats. This happened to be very hazardous duty since the Germans would send up flares that would light up the sky until it looked like daylight. Then our patrols were sitting ducks.

These patrols had to be canceled because of numerous casualties. The Germans were perched on high ground and could observe every movement of our night patrols.

After a few weeks of relative quiet on the west bank of the Rhine River it was time to get ready for the crossing. Dummy tanks and other military equipment partially camouflaged were placed at various strategic points to confuse the enemy. The exact crossing was to be kept a secret from the Germans. Numerous movements of military traffic all along the river were carried out to further confuse the enemy.

The Rhine crossing by the 102nd Infantry Division was scheduled to begin the first week of March. Since most of the bridges were damaged or destroyed it was necessary for the engineers to build a pontoon bridge for the major crossing. Anti-aircraft guns and other artillery were concentrated near the crossing to protect the troops and military vehicles.

The Rhine River crossing was the last major obstacle to overcome in order for our tanks and other mechanized equipment to pursue the German armies to Berlin.

POLITICS REARS HEAD DURING WWII
Sunday, October 17, 1999

In the first week of March 1945 our infantry troops made the initial crossing of the Rhine at Remagen. A railroad bridge was still intact and our infantry troops took advantage of this crossing.

Patrols were first sent out to determine what the German defenses were. Since very little opposition was met, our infantry kept building up the troop strength in this area. The Germans didn't expect any large scale battles in the area because of the lack of major roads or other military targets.

The major troop crossing of the 102nd Infantry Division across the Rhine River took place the first week of April 1945. The location was several miles north of the Krefeld area. Pontoon bridges were built at several locations to accommodate all the military traffic which included all sizes of trucks, tanks and other military equipment.

All available anti-aircraft guns were positioned near these bridges to protect our troops during the crossing from German aircraft. Our Air Force was also called on to protect the troops at these crossings.

Our unit was alerted to make a night crossing several days after the initial crossing. A buddy of mine and I packed our belongings in a Volkswagen that we "requisitioned" to make this trip. When we got to the pontoon bridge we were stopped by the military police. We were told that since our vehicle was too narrow to fit on the pontoon bridge we could not cross. We were told to go south a few miles to a place where another crossing was available to accommodate our vehicle.

We were driving at night under blackout conditions and didn't have any idea where we were supposed to meet our unit across the Rhine. We drove several miles before we found the place to cross with our narrow gage vehicle. We had no idea where we were or where we were going. About two days later we managed to find our headquarters.

For the next three weeks the Army was moving five to 10 miles a day. The armored units lead the way clearing out the main roads. The infantry had the task of mopping up the flanks. There were numerous individual battles between the infantry and the German units. Some of the die-hard SS (Elite) troops fought until they were totally eliminated.

Germans were coming out of the bushes with white flags ready to surrender. Hundreds of Germans were surrendering everyday. Some of our troops were caught up in the fast moving effort and were captured. Most of our prisoners were released in a few days when our reinforcements caught up with our infantry.

The nearer we got to Berlin the more German units were willing to surrender. The number increased from hundreds to thousands. The Germans were getting weary and were ready for their part of the war to end. They were marched though the streets and highways to hastily fenced compounds.

We finally reached the Elbe River about the 20th of April. Our infantry sent patrols across the river to determine what German units would be encountered. We were about 50 miles from Berlin.

Our infantry was located near Tangermunde on the Elbe River. A major bridge at the location was partially destroyed some weeks before by our Air Force. A German commander in charge of the major military units on the east side of the Elbe River asked to surrender his troops. His only request was permission to repair enough of the bridge to provide a walkway for his troops to surrender. This request was granted.

As the Germans reached the west side of the river they were instructed to drop all their weapons and military equipment and march down the highway in a column of twos. The surrender took place 24 hours a day for several days. The weapons were piled several feet high when we managed to get to this location. We were authorized to take one pistol only and were cautioned that all the weapons were loaded. I managed to get a German Luger which was considered the best military pistol the Germans made.

I later traded my Luger for a Belgium P-35 and an electric razor. This was a very stupid thing to do. I didn't realize how valuable the Luger was. I was interested in shaving with an electric razor (also battery operated) since my face was raw from shaving several days growth of beard with cold water and soap.

The Russians were about 30 miles from the Elbe River and we could hear their artillery coming into the area where the remnants of the German army was located. The Germans feared the Russians and didn't want to be captured by them. They knew they would be sent to Siberia if they were captured.

Our armies were not authorized to go beyond the Elbe River and on to Berlin since this decision was made at Yalta by the "Big Three." At the Yalta meeting it was decided that we would let the Russians take Berlin since it would be a tremendous morale booster for the Russian armies. The "Big Three" was composed of Franklin D. Roosevelt, Joseph Stalin and Winston Churchill. Many bad decisions were made at the Yalta meeting and we lived to regret them.

GIs Sold Watches To Russian Soldiers
Sunday, December 19, 1999

The Russians finally reached the Elbe River about the end of April 1945 and met with our troops all along the river.

It was a joyous occasion for the Allies and the Russians. I am sure it meant more to the Russians since they had been at war for several years fighting the Germans. They were fighting the Germans all along the borders and in the heart of the homeland.

Now it was time to celebrate the happy occasion with our troops who had waited several days at the Elbe River for their arrival. The meeting of the victorious ranking officers of both armies was high-lighted by the news media all over the world. However, the rank and file also had their day toasting each other with vodka, Schnapps and anything else that was available.

Numerous get-togethers were held by all of the Allied and Russian units that were stationed along the borders of both armies. The parties continued for several days. Very few Russians could speak English and very few GIs could speak Russian. However, that did not diminish the enthusiasm that these meetings brought about.

I had the privilege of attending one of the functions at a club that was organized by officers of my unit. The Russians sent their hand picked officers (men and women) so that they could make a very good impression on our military.

Finally all the celebrations came to an end and in a few days our division was ordered to move to a different area. This came about without much advance notice and it developed into mass confusion for a few days. It seemed like our area of occupation was determined months before by the Big Three and their staff of politicians at the Yalta meeting.

It seemed like things changed overnight. The Russians setup roadblocks on their borders with machine guns placed at strategic locations. The friendly atmosphere no longer existed. The Russians evicted the civilians from their homes without any advance notice so that their troops could have living quarters in their area of occupation.

When we were finally settled in our official occupation area, we had to place guards at our borders to patrol the area. The Russian guards were just a short distance from our location. In some areas we used guards on horseback to patrol the border. Of course the horses were formerly used by the German military during the war.

These horses were "requisitioned" by our troops and were used as long as we remained in this area.

It did not take long for our GIs to get friendly with the Russian guards. Bartering between the troops was an everyday affair.

The Russian military had not been paid their military pay for the entire period of service. Some of these troops had three to five years pay due them. Eventually, they were paid all of their back pay and it didn't take long for our GIs to find this out. One of the things that every Russian soldier dreamed of was owning an American watch.

Our GIs were sending urgent messages home to have their folks send them all the cheap watches they could buy. The $5 Mickey Mouse watches were in great demand. The going price was $100. Thousands of these watches were sold to the Russian troops. They felt like a "King for a Day" if they had a watch!

Eventually the supply of watches from back home was exhausted. One enterprising GI had a brilliant idea. He would make a sundial and sell it to the Russian soldiers who didn't have a watch. He managed to find a relatively neat looking stick that he used to make a circle in the loamy soil. He then placed the stick in the center of the circle. The shadow made by the stick on the edge of the circle would be used to determine the present hour. Then the remaining hours would be placed onto the circle in an appropriate location. The sundial was now complete and ready for sale. The magic stick was then sold for the going price of $100.

I have often wondered what the Russian soldier thought when the magic stick didn't work for him. Of course that GI never showed his face and I am sure he left that area to never return again.

LOT OF BARTERING DONE DURING WARTIME
Sunday, March 5, 2000

Occupation began at the end of hostilities in April 1945. Thousands of prisoners, displaced persons and various transients had to be fed, housed and cared for until final disposition was made by our military government.

Gen. Keating, commanding general of the 102nd Infantry Division was declared the military governor of the area occupied by the 102nd Infantry Division. It took months to resolve many of the problems that faced our military government. What a nightmare!

There were isolated cases of German youth groups trying to stir up trouble. Some die-hard Nazis also caused problems but all these groups were soon quelled. We slept with our pistols and rifles loaded and ready in case we needed them in a hurry. The majority of the Germans were glad the war was over and they were ready to cooperate with us.

Our temporary occupation areas were soon replaced with more permanent occupation areas and things began to get down to a more normal routine. Our troops were assigned housing facilities that were available in the area. Kitchen facilities and other military facilities were placed in service. Existing buildings and homes were used for this purpose.

By agreement of our military government with the local German government, we were authorized to hire kitchen help and other necessary help to do certain chores. These people were paid by the local

German government with pay based on current hourly wages. This was part of the reparation agreement worked out by our military with the German government. I never did understand this arrangement, but these were political decisions over which we had no control.

It was my responsibility to pay these civilian employees at the end of the month. On or about the last day of the month, I would report to the courthouse to pick up the pay. The payroll complete with names, job titles and pay scale would be ready for me to deliver. I was the paymaster for all the batteries of our battalion and it took me a couple days to locate the employees at the various battery locations to pay them. This was a happy occasion for these employees since jobs were hard to come by.

Occupation duties consisted primarily of necessary guard duty and routine maintenance and normal military duty. Organized athletics were carried out daily to keep morale at a high pitch.

Local brewmasters were located and arrangements were made to have beer available for the troops. Most every village had a brewmaster and usually they were very cooperative. Yeast was a scarce item, so we would take the brewmaster to the nearest town to scout the black market to buy yeast. We would give the brewmaster a part of the yeast for his efforts and that satisfied him.

The 102nd Division Band was relieved of most of their normal military duties so that they could entertain the troops at night. The troops enjoyed the music as they sipped on their bottles of local beer. The music of the 40s played by the band, certainly made you homesick. If you wanted to cry in your beer, you had plenty of buddies to share in your thoughts of loved ones back home.

We learned that deer was available in the general area where we were located. It didn't take long for our GI deer hunters to round up a few of their buddies and go hunting. There was plenty of deer available and our hunters would always bring in two or three each time. Usually the local butcher would clean the deer and prepare it for our cook. The meal was a real treat for our troops.

A locally-owned German bakery was located near our quarters. We traded our beer for some homemade bread occasionally. The bread was made from imitation flour, but it tasted okay.

Practically all local foods were made from imitation ingredients which was refereed to as ERSATZ. The flour at the bakery was made from sawdust, we were told. ERSATZ coffee looked like weak tea. It looked like it was made from wood pellets. We lived off GI rations and did not partake of the local German fare very often. Real food was hard to come by.

We did a lot of bartering with the local folks. Cigarettes were as valuable as gold. A pack of cigarettes could buy a 100 pound sack of potatoes during potato harvest. Semi-precious jewelry could be bought for a pack of cigarettes.

Domestic help would be glad to clean the quarters, shine shoes or do odd jobs for a few cigarettes. Of course, we used some German currency once in a while if our cigarette supply was exhausted. Most of us still had some German currency that we had accumulated from various sources during our trek through Germany.

The local folks would rarely accept our military invasion currency. We were paid with this scrip since American money was not authorized to be used. New scrip was issued in each country that we were located at during our stay. It was not unusual to have your billfold with French francs, German marks and Dutch guilder scrip. You would also accumulate other currencies if you had occasion to visit other countries during your tour of duty.

ATTENTION TO MONEY NEEDED WHEN GIS PLANNING TO TRAVEL
Sunday, May 14, 2000

The military government was responsible for printing of the scrip that was used by the American troops stationed in Europe. The military pay was in the form of scrip which was also called "invasion money."

The local Germans would accept this scrip for payment of purchases by our troops but would rather accept payment in German currency. Every GI had accumulated some German currency and didn't expect it to have any value after the war was over.

Most of the troops planned to take it home as a souvenir. German marcs were treated as worthless paper until we found out it did have some value.

During the bartering that went on with the Russian soldiers, we suddenly realized that the Russians were using the same scrip as we were. The only difference was a dash before the serial number. Our finance officer would not accept this scrip that the Russians were using. Apparently he was not advised about this currency.

Our military government must have had some sort of agreement with the Russian military government to use our equipment to print their currency. Eventually word got to our finance people to accept the Russian currency. I'm sure politics were involved in this arrangement and as usual, our government lost a fortune because of this questionable arrangement with the Russians.

Black marketing was going on in most all of the towns where our troops were stationed. Some of our soldiers accumulated large sums of money from these activities. It seems that almost every soldier had extra scrip that he managed to get through various dealings with the local fellas and others. Some made fortunes from gambling with the troops.

Now was the time to send the money home before you had chance to blow it on some foolish endeavor. Money orders through the military post office was the only way you could send money home.

However, because of the black marketing, you were restricted to sending home only the amount you received from your monthly pay. The military was determined to stop the black marketing and this decision just about stopped this problem.

Fortunes were made by many GIs before the restrictions were put into force. Gambling and bartering accounted for large sums of money that was sent home. I recall a Jeep driver who told me he sent home more than $20,000 to his mother for safe keeping until he got home.

Arrangements were made by our military to authorize leaves of absence to London, the Riviera, Paris and Switzerland. Quotas were established for each unit to visit these vacation areas. Lists were prepared and priorities were sent by the various organizations. There was a limit on the amount of money that could be converted to be spent at each vacation resort.

I had an opportunity to go to the Riviera (Southern France), but I declined since I was waiting to go to Switzerland. Everyone who went to Switzerland came back with interesting stories about their trips. A limit of $35 was all that could be converted to use for this trip.

All those who planned to take this trip were advised by their buddies to take all the GI raincoats they could get. Raincoats were apparently a very scarce item there, although no one had ever mentioned that it rained while they were there. Everyone returned with two or three Swiss watches. The $35 went a long way if you had a couple of raincoats to barter with.

Back at our quarters in the village of Housenburg in the Bavarian Alps, things were back to a normal routine. After our evening meal we would gather at our favorite meeting place adjacent to our quarters and reminisce about the folks back home while enjoying a cool glass of local beer. Occasionally some local talent would be invited in to entertain us.

There were two former members of a German concert orchestra who came by one evening. One played the violin and the other played the piano. They played a couple of their concert songs for us and you could tell they were read professionals.

We taught them a couple of songs which they learned in a few minutes. All you had to do was hum a song and the piano player would write the notes down on his music sheet. He would then play the song one time and would make any corrections we suggested.

After some chatting in German, they would be ready to play. And play they did! They added all the frills and made it sound like a concert number that they had played for a long time. What a talent!

My buddy Bill invited me to go on a boat ride on the Danube River at Passau, which was a short distance from our quarters. He had managed to find a boat with a small motor that we were going to use for this trip. It was a beautiful summer day when we put the boat into the Danube River. The motor started on the first try and we were off on the cruise of the beautiful blue Danube River. Several minutes later the motor started to sputter and finally quit.

We tried to start the motor and it wouldn't do a thing. The river had a swift current that took us down stream in a hurry. We would soon be approaching the locks and it would tear our boat to pieces. Fortunately, a large cruiser was anchored nearby. The sailors saw that we were in trouble so they lowered some long poles that we grabbed and were pulled to safety on the deck of their boat. Our guardian angels came to our rescue one more time and we thank God for that.

EUROPEAN WAR END CAUSES MOVEMENT OF AMERICAN TROOPS
Sunday, July 16, 2000

Since the war in Europe was over in May 1945, the troops were concerned about being sent to the Pacific to engage the enemy in that theater of operations.

Some units were being sent back to the States for a few days of vacation and then on to the Pacific combat area. We were fortunate in that our division was scheduled to be deactivated in the not too distant future.

The point system was used to determine how soon you were eligible to be returned to the States. The points were established by your years of active service, time spent in a combat area, military awards for bravery and meritorious service in a combat zone. If you accumulated 90-100 points, you would be eligible to be considered for an early trip back to the States.

I had amassed 95 points since I had five years and three months of active service, nine months in a combat zone, 16 months overseas and one Bronze Star Medal for meritorious service.

Priority for the trip back to the States was given to units scheduled for duty in the Pacific. Some units were sent directly to the Pacific area without stopping off at the States.

Transportation was a very serious problem. Passenger ships were used that could carry approximately 5,000 personnel.

The *Queen Mary* with a capacity of 30,000 troops, was also placed into service to carry troops. This ship was used to carry troops to England before we entered the war in Europe. The *Queen Mary* could outrun any submarine that the Germans used. It could make the trip from New York to England in three to 3-1/2 days.

Victory ships were also put into service to carry troops back to the

October 1945

States. These ships were made to carry freight and could accommodate 100-200 troops. The trips across the Atlantic took 12-15 days. It was a rough ride!

Troop movement to the Pacific area continued until August 1945. President Truman made a very bold decision to use the atom bomb at the heart of Japan. The first bomb was dropped on Hiroshima which killed thousands of Japanese and injured thousands more in addition to the total destruction of homes and businesses.

The Japanese government would not agree to surrender and the decision was name to drop the second atom bomb on Nagasaki. The Japanese government finally came to its senses and accepted the unconditional surrender terms.

An invasion of Japan was planned by the military before the atom bombing was considered. I'm sure very few top military commanders were aware of the existence of the atom bomb. The use of the atom bomb saved the invasion of the Japanese homeland, which would have cost hundreds of thousands of casualties. Thank God for the atom bomb. War is hell and there are no winners.

After considering the occupation duties we were performing, one felt very fortunate in that we didn't have to be sent to the Pacific. Of course, we were very anxious to be sent back to the States since we were away from our families for more than 16 months.

Various educational programs were made available to those who were interested. Some took advantage of machine shop training in towns where this equipment was available. Others took advantage of various educational opportunities.

Bavaria was noted for manufacturing of various types of chinaware. All we had to do was make arrangements with these factories and supply them with coal to fire up their ovens. Many of the troops bought this chinaware and had it sent home.

We even made arrangements to have our battalion insignia placed on a set of china to be sent home. Many of my buddies received their china after we returned to the States. Mine never arrived, but I think the post office failed to forward mine after I moved to a different address.

Local tailor shops would make most anything as long as you provided the materials. Cloth was a scarce item, but many of the GIs managed to find what they needed to make riding trousers and other items. I had a couple pair of boots made by a local shoemaker after I managed to get the shoe leather for this project. Germans were masters of various trades and we took advantage of all of their skills.

Transportation was almost non-existent for the local folks. Old busses that were using coal-fired engines were seen occasionally in the larger towns. It wasn't unusual to see a bus stop along the roadside with the driver stoking the fire in the rear (outside) of the bus. Gasoline for the locals was non-existent.

Occasionally you would see an old farm tractor (1920 vintage) dragging several trailers through town loaded with people and supplies. Huge Belgium horses would usually be seen in the rural areas with wagons loaded with all sorts of farm tools and supplies.

These horses would be frightened by any military vehicle that happened to pass by. We have seen the horses takeoff across the countryside after being frightened by one of our vehicles.

It was hard to believe that a nation so far advanced in military armament that included jet aircraft and guided missiles, yet was still using ancient farm equipment to plow their fields.

ENTERTAINMENT HELPED KEEP MORALE HIGH AFTER VE DAY
Sunday, August 27, 2000

The surrender of Japan in August 1945 was the news we had hoped and prayed for while doing occupation duties in Germany. We felt that our trip back home could become a reality in the not-too-distant future.

To keep the morale at a high pitch, all sorts of activities were planned to keep the troops happy. Organized athletics were to be carried out on a daily basis. Volleyball was one of my favorite sports. The team that had the tallest men usually won the games. It really didn't matter who won as long as we were having fun.

Horseback riding was also very popular with some of the troops, especially those who lived in rural areas. Drugstore cowboys even enjoyed the sport of kings. Military horses were rounded up and used for this purpose. All military horses were branded with the Nazi insignia on their legs. These horses would probably never qualify to run in the Kentucky Derby, but they served their purpose.

Entertainment of the troops was high on the agenda also. We rarely had an opportunity to be entertained by Hollywood talent from the States. I guess Bob Hope and his troupe spent all their time roaming the Pacific Theater of Operations and entertaining the troops in many of the far flung islands.

Our 102nd Infantry Division Band became active shortly after the war in Germany was over in May 1945. Most of the band members were doing duty as cooks and dining personnel in rear echelon areas during the war. I'm sure they were glad to be active in the band again.

All the band instruments and items of uniforms and other non-essential items were stored in a cave in France during the war. Guards were assigned to this duty and I'm sure they were envied by the combat soldiers.

The 102nd Infantry Division Band played songs of the Big Band Era (1930-40) and were enjoyed by all the GIs. They performed for our 380th FA Battalion on several occasions. Beer was available during these concerts and it was not unusual to see the GIs cry in their beer. The songs they played brought back memories and made many folks homesick.

A popular European circus performed for our troops on one occasion. Since this performance was held some distance from our unit, only a few of our GIs had an opportunity to attend this performance.

Once in a while some talented (European) groups would come to our area. We had a magician perform for us and he was a big hit. He would walk out into the crowd and get a cigarette from one of the GIs. He would mark the cigarette, light it and go back on stage. After a few puffs, the cigarette would disappear. Then he would go back to the audience and pluck the cigarette from some GI's pocket.

The next trick he performed was the "bake the cake trick." He would get a GI helmet liner from the audience. Then back on stage he would put in a couple of eggs, flour and milk and stir it up. He would let it set for a few minutes while he got busy doing other things on the stage.

He couldn't speak English, so I would interpret for him. He was Hungarian and I learned to speak Hungarian from my parents, who were born in Hungary. Now, it was time to check the cake. He brought the helmet liner with the cake mixture to a table on stage, flipped it over and there it was, a beautiful cake ready to eat.

A gentleman with a beautiful tenor voice happened to be in one of the troops that performed for us. We taught him the "Indian Love Song." He couldn't speak a word of English, but he learned the words to the song and did a magnificent job of signing that beautiful song. What a talent!

We would spend our nights sitting around sipping beer and trying to chase the blues. Some of the guys would get together and sing some of the old songs of the 30s and 40s. We had a lot of GIs who were really talented but didn't have an opportunity to use it. One of these GIs wrote a song which expressed our feelings. This song was sung to the tune of *"Lily Marlene:"*

Oh, Mr. Truman, why can't we go home?
We have conquered Naples, we have conquered Rome.
We have mastered the master race,
Oh, why can't we have shipping space?
Oh, Mr. Truman, why can't we go home?

I often wondered what President Truman thought if he heard this song.

MAKING FRIENDS IN HOLLAND
Sunday, October 15, 2000

The 102nd Infantry Division landed in France about the 24th of September 1944. After a few days of orientation, the infantry units were sent to Herleen, Holland located on the border of Holland and Germany. They were assigned to existing infantry units for combat experience.

Most of the artillery units were assigned duties as "Red Ball Express" to haul supplies from Cherbourg to Paris. All the combat units would get their supplies from the warehouse in Paris.

The 380th Field Artillery Battalion was assigned duties on the Red Ball Express. Every member of the battalion who didn't have guard duty or other administrative duties was assigned as a driver or assistant driver with a 2-1/2 ton GI truck. Some of the GIs never drove a truck in their lives but had to learn in a hurry.

The trucks rolled 24 hours a day. The drivers would take turns resting so the convoys could keep rolling. About the third day the convoys would stop at their headquarters, located about midway between the port and Paris. The drivers would have an opportunity to clean up and rest a few hours and get ready for the next trip.

The Allies had driven the Germans out of Paris and other areas of France and were approaching the permanent fortification of the Siegfried Line. The Red Ball Express was doing a great job of getting the supplies from the port at Cherbourg to a central location in Paris. The supply problem was critical and the Red Ball Express did a great job of supplying the advancing troops.

After about 30 days, our battalion was relieved of this duty and given orders to proceed to Herleen, Holland. We traveled by GI trucks and reached our destination a few days later. We arrived at night and were assigned quarters at an old schoolhouse.

Before we had a chance to settle down for the night, anti-aircraft guns which were located in the school yard, started firing at enemy planes. It sounded like all hell broke loose and scared us since we didn't know there were any guns anywhere nearby. Some of the guys started to dig foxholes for protection from the enemy aircraft and artillery.

We were glad to see the sunrise and get over our initial shock. We suddenly realized that we were at war and not on a training maneuver back in the States. We setup our kitchen on one of the streets and assigned quarters to the troops. We were given guard duties and other routine duties for the next few days.

We lined up for chow in the street since our kitchen facilities were in operation. Children of the town came by at mealtime with their tin buckets hoping to get some of the leftovers after each meal. There always were leftovers and our cooks were glad to share the food with these children who took them home to share them with their families. Food was scarce since the Germans took whatever food was available during their occupation of Holland.

We looked forward to seeing these children each day. We shared everything we got from home with them. We always managed to have candy and chewing gum to give to these children. Almost all of them could speak English and they knew several songs that some of the GIs taught them.

The people of Holland were very friendly. We made arrangements with local families to have our clothes washed while we were stationed in Herleen. We were authorized to use the bathing facilities (showers) that the coal miners used after their shift in the mines. They were glad to see us and they were proud to share everything they had.

Our 102nd Infantry Division became good friends of the people of Herleen, Holland. Our division formed the 102nd Infantry Division Association while we were doing occupation duties in Germany. Since the war, reunions are held annually with locations determined by vote during the meetings held at the reunions. The mayor of Herleen or his representatives attend these annual reunions.

Trips are scheduled to return to Herleen every couple of years. The entire town celebrates the return of our division. Many friends have been made at these reunions and they all look forward to seeing each other. Lifetime friendships are priceless.

A few weeks after Herleen was liberated, our division was being readied to advance into Germany. The British troops were located at our left flank and were to coordinate their movements with our division. It seems that the British troops were never ready to move at the appointed hour. There always seemed to be a communication problem.

After some delay, the timing of the movement of British and American troops was resolved and the advance toward the Siegfried Line had begun. It didn't take long to realize that we were involved in the greatest war the European continent had ever experienced.

War is hell and no truer words were ever spoken.

Most Just Happy To Get Home After War To Be With Families

The first week of November 1944, the entire 102nd Infantry Division was committed into combat in the Siegfried Line. The front line extended into Germany, a short distance from the Holland border.

The movement of troops was hampered by rain during most of the month of November. Some of the secondary roads were turned into a sea of mud and made it almost impossible to get supplies to our troops.

The fortifications of the Siegfried Line were made up of reinforced concrete bunkers and pillboxes located mostly on high ground. The flat and rolling countryside was covered with minefields. Tank traps consisted of trenches dug about 10 feet wide and eight feet deep. This made the advancement of armored vehicles, tanks and other equipment almost impossible. The main roads were zeroed in by the Germans so that their artillery could fire at any movement of our military vehicles.

The Siegfried Line covered an area from the Swiss frontier to the Holland border. Most of the permanent fortifications were built about 1940. The trenches and tank traps were built mostly by civilians and prisoners who were forced to carry out this work by the German military. Most of this work was done a short time before our armies invaded Germany.

It was very difficult to keep track of the days since being in a combat zone, because more important things were on your mind. Important days like family birthdays, holidays and other important events were dismissed from your mind.

When snow began to fall about the first of December, you couldn't help but think of Christmas. Your thoughts turned to past Christmases back home with family and friends. The snow covered trees, field and roads were constant reminders of the scenic landscape back home.

I remember seeing an elderly lady dressed in black tromping through the knee-deep snow. I wondered where she came from and where she was going. The civilians all fled as the armies approached and all the villages and towns were deserted as our armies moved forward into their homeland.

The Christmas spirit was alive and well in areas where actual combat slowed down for the Christmas holidays. There were very few special meals for most of the GIs and even K-rations were a treat during the temporary lull in combat activities.

Some of the GIs managed to find small trees that were used as Christmas trees. If you had a shelter to keep them out of the weather, you could even manage to make a few decorations out of scraps of leaves and paper and other wrappings from home.

Thoughts of Christmas at home were on your mind and everyone hoped that the war would soon end. We were all very thankful that we lived to see this Christmas and hoped to be home for the next one.

On Christmas day, combat operations slowed down by the Germans in our area and our troops remained on alert with only a few firing missions. It was an opportunity for some of our troops to visit their buddies in nearby units. The ground was covered with snow and it was difficult to do much traveling under those conditions.

I remember Lt. Sam Epstein from Service Battery, 380th Field Artillery Battalion, visiting our battalion headquarters. As he came down the steps into the basement where our headquarters were located, he slipped down the snow-covered stairs and landed at the bottom of the stairs. He was carried to our aid station where it was determined that he had a broken leg. His injury was classified as a million dollar wound and got him a one-way ticket back home.

Sam was a likable person and we would have all been glad to trade places with him. After the war, we heard from him from his home in Houston. He was a real estate broker and I guess he got active again in his real estate business. Eventually he moved to New York and we lost track of him.

I'm sure we all secretly wished for a million dollar wound, but we are happy that we made it back home after the war to enjoy many more Christmases with our families and friends. Thank God for that.

SOME SOLDIERS NEVER RETURNED HOME FROM WAR
Sunday, January 28, 2001

Palenberg was the first town inside Germany, a short distance from the Holland border that was to be our home for the next several weeks. This was a coal mining area. It was also the Siegfried Line area that the Germans had fortified and planned to defend at all cost.

We were headquartered in an old mine administration building that had been bombed by our Air Force sometime ago. This was a multi-story structure that was better than staying in a camouflaged makeshift shelter.

Guards were posted at various entrances for the protection of the troops. These were Dutch soldiers who were assigned duties by some agreement with our military. A Dutch officer was in charge of these guards. None of these soldiers could speak English and they had to call on their officer in charge to resolve any communication problem.

Our artillery units were located some distance from our headquarters and it became necessary for me to make trips to visit our battalion commander to transact routine and other military business. I would usually get a message by radio or by messenger to report to Col. Hannigan, our battalion commander. A Jeep with driver was usually available for these trips. Our battalion headquarters was usually located in a basement at a bombed out building some distance from any road. We would follow the telephone lines (lying on the ground) and some makeshift military signs identifying our battalion location.

The battalion fire direction center was located in a basement where orders were given by radio to fire at various targets. Forward observers, located at strategic locations usually on high ground, rooftops or church steeples, would send messages to the fire direction center to make whatever corrections to hit the targets. The 105 Howitzers were located somewhere between the fire director center and the forward observer location.

Artillery aircraft with pilot and forward observer would also assist in locating these targets. The artillery planes could cruise at about 120 mph and stay in the air for several hours. They could locate enemy gun positions and enemy troop movement that could not be seen by the forward observers from their ground locations.

We were very fortunate in having only a few casualties of all the hundreds of hours that the artillery planes were in the air. One of these planes was attacked by a German fighter but managed to escape being hit by out maneuvering the German plane. The enemy aircraft going about 500 mph was too fast to out maneuver these artillery planes that could make abrupt turns since they were going slow compared to the enemy planes. Our artillery planes were also subjected to small arms fire and enemy artillery fire but managed to escape most of these hazards.

Back on the ground our infantry had the toughest job of fighting the enemy. The permanent fortifications of the Siegfried Line were a constant challenge. Enemy machine guns were always located on high ground where they had a perfect view at any activity of our troops. Crossing the beet fields was most hazardous because of land mines that were everywhere. The German 88s were zeroed in on all the major roads and intersections.

Patrols were sent out at night to determine where the enemy was located and any other military intelligence that they could bring back from these patrols. Capturing a prisoner was also a very important part of the mission of these patrols. Of course, coming back with all your patrol without serious injury or casualties was of utmost importance.

Interrogating these prisoners by our military intelligence people would help to determine what action would be taken by our commanders. Knowing where the enemy units were located and the type and number of troops was of utmost importance. Our commanders made decisions based on the information obtained from the prisoners and other military intelligence.

The advance of our troops into enemy territory required coordination of all infantry and artillery units in the area. The gaining of ground was measured by yards in the heavily fortified Siegfried Line. The use of hand grenades and hand-to-hand fighting was necessary to flush out the enemy from their entrenched positions.

There were many heroes in each of these engagements with the enemy. Some of these heroes managed to survive and many others didn't make it. Many of the heroes didn't get the recognition they deserved.

Some of these GIs became mental casualties and had to be sent back to field hospitals and eventually to permanent hospitals in the States. Many who survived are still being cared for in VA hospitals and will never get over their illnesses. This is how terrible war is and there are no winners.

Many of the soldiers are buried in cemeteries in Holland. Some have returned home for their final resting place.

FRENCH GOVERNMENT QUICKLY BECAME INDIFFERENT TO FORCES
Sunday, March 4, 2001

We landed in Cherbourg on or about September 23, 1944 after about a six-hour trip across the English Channel from a port in southern England. We spent a couple of days near the village of St. Mere Eglise using pup tents during our temporary stay. Of course, it rained constantly and we were glad when we got orders to leave this area.

The village had cobblestone streets with a creek running through the edge of town. We saw elderly women washing clothes on the creek bank. We couldn't believe that such primitive behavior was still going on in a civilized country.

As we rode through the village in GI trucks, people stood at the edge of the streets waving at us as our convoy drove by. Some were praying and were thankful that our armies had liberated their area from the Germans.

We had received orders to make arrangements to start hauling supplies from the port to Paris. Our entire battalion was assigned duties as the Red Ball Express. Enough 2-1/2 ton trucks were assigned to us to use every available man in our battalion to drive these trucks. Each driver had an assistant who would take over to relieve him since these trucks would run 24 hours each day. There was an urgent need for supplies by our advancing armies.

In order to limit traffic problems, a one-way route (two lanes) was used from the port to Paris and an alternate route was used for the return trip from Paris to the port. Our headquarters was located about mid-point. About once a week the drivers were given a day or so to clean up and get some rest.

We stayed in a building that looked like a castle. There was no one living there so we decided to set up our headquarters there. After a few days the owner shows up and we had to vacate the place to find other quarters. Some of these people seemed to forget that our armies had just run the Germans out of their homes and gave them their freedom.

Most of the French people were glad that we were there since they were living under Nazi rule for a long time. The French government became very indifferent a short while after they received their freedom. They didn't need us anymore. They put up with our military for a couple of years and they let our government know that they wanted us to vacate all the buildings in Paris and other areas and leave.

We were forced to move our troops out of their country. After the war, Gen. DeGaulle didn't remember that we saved their country in WWI and also in WWII. He was a very arrogant political character who stayed in power for several years.

Local women who fraternized with the German soldiers during occupation were singled out and had their heads shaved. Germany sympathizers were also rounded up and disciplined.

Many French property owners made claims against our military for various minor damages caused by military vehicles driving through the narrow cobblestone streets. People get greedy when money is involved.

Our tour of duty with the Red Ball Express ended after about two months and we were on our way to join our combat forces on the border of Holland and Germany.

A couple of days before we departed, I received orders from my commanding officer, Col. Hannigan, to find three of our men from Service Battery, 380th Field Artillery, who were unaccounted for as we prepared to move. I made the rounds of all the military police headquarters in Paris to see if they had any records of our missing soldiers.

We finally found the names of these men on one of the rosters at the military police headquarters in Paris. I was advised to go to a former French prison near the south outskirts of Paris that was used by our military to house military prisoners.

My Jeep driver and I managed to get lost on our way but somehow we finally found the ancient prison that housed our three missing soldiers. After some discussion with the military prison authorities, they released our long-lost soldiers. They looked like they hadn't bathed or shaved in several days. We were glad to see them and they were certainly glad to see us.

We questioned our prisoners to determine what they had done to be placed in prison. They claimed that the French police who were guarding the warehouse where our military supplies were being stored in Paris accused them of trying to steal some supplies. No formal charges were filed and they were imprisoned because of some administrative foul-up.

I'm sure there was more to this story, but I never did get anymore facts from our three Service Battery soldiers. I didn't remember their names and I would like to hear from them and get the entire story.

We started back to our headquarters and was glad to report to Col. Hannigan that our mission was successful and we were ready to start our trip to the combat area near the Holland-German border.

TRAVEL CONDITIONS HAMPERED DURING FALL, WINTER MONTHS
Sunday, April 15, 2001

Rains during the fall and winter months of 1945 hampered the movement of troops along the entire front. Since a large part of the traveling was done cross-country and on dirt makeshift roads, very little progress was made.

Movement of artillery guns, tanks and other heavy equipment was very difficult under these conditions. The engineers worked constantly, repairing trails and roads in the sea of mud. The four-wheel drive of these military vehicles helped to overcome some of these mud-clogged roads.

The hauling of gasoline, ammunition, food and other supplies had to continue during these rainy days. Vehicles that were stalled or stuck in the mud had to be towed to the nearest truck maintenance areas. Incoming artillery continued regardless of the weather and it wasn't unusual to have vehicles and equipment damaged or destroyed under these conditions. Personnel casualties increased since they were exposed to the incoming artillery.

I often wondered what happened to the civilians who lived in these areas. They had to leave their homes without any advance notice and run for their lives. It was not unusual to find a cow or hog or chickens in an abandoned farmhouse.

Most of these animals were on the menu the next day if our cooks were available in these areas. Our battalion medical officer would inspect the animals and give the okay to prepare the food for the troops.

There were many farm animals that were caught by the incoming artillery and were usually killed instantly. It was not unusual to locate these animals since the stench was beyond description. When the cows died, they would lay on their back with their feet straight up in the air. If we were driving by these dead animals, we would turn on the speed and get out of the area as fast as we could.

More tanks and other military vehicles and equipment kept moving up to the front lines. We were glad to see them and waved as they passed by. The tank hatches were open and the GIs would wave back at us.

I recognized one of the GIs in the tank who waved back to us. I couldn't believe I actually saw someone from my hometown. I don't know if he recognized me. It was Alex Baranyl, a friend I had known practically all my life. I never had the occasion to meet him after the war to talk to him about this occasion.

I remember seeing signs at various crossroads that some GIs had placed on trees or poles that read "5,210 miles to Austin, Texas" or "5,000 to USA." I also remember seeing signs in some of the most remote areas that read "Kilroy was here." I don't know who Kilroy was, but he sure managed to get around. I couldn't believe he could get around to so many places. I'll bet every GI in the combat zones of Germany had seen his sign, "Kilroy was here."

While we were stationed at the old coal mine building in Palenberg, we had a semi-permanent kitchen setup at our headquarters. We usually had two cooked meals a day. Powered eggs and toast was a typical breakfast.

The eggs weren't too bad if you put a lot of salt on them to give them a better taste. We usually had C-ration stew for the evening meal. It was rumored that this was made with kangaroo meat from Australia. If you were hungry, it didn't taste too bad.

We always had K-rations in reserve. They were boxed in a paper container the size of a Cracker Jack box. They had meals for breakfast and lunch. The breakfast box contained a small can of scrambled eggs, two hard tack crackers and a small pack of cigarettes. The cigarettes varied from Lucky Strike, Camels and some other brands. There were four cigarettes in each box.

The lunch K-ration contained a small can of cheese or Spam and a piece of unsweetened chocolate. The chocolate was impossible to chew, so we would cut off a piece with a knife and let it melt in our mouths for a few hours. We would eat this chocolate only as a last resort.

If you ran out of food and were very hungry, you would always have a piece of chocolate in your knapsack. The K-rations were issued to you if you were on the move for a few days and the kitchen facilities were not available.

Water was usually available as long as you were not on the move. Your canteen held about a pint of water. The engineers always managed to find water and purify it for the troops. If you happened to run out of water and were not near any locations that had a supply, you could use local water sources.

You better use your halazone tablets (two to a canteen of water) or face the possibility of getting diarrhea or other more terrible ailments. The halazone tablets made the water look soapy and taste awful, but it could keep you from dying of thirst.

As the war progressed, so did the casualties. Grave registration teams came around periodically to pick up the fallen soldiers. They were placed on the 2-1/2 ton GI trucks and taken to temporary headquarters where they were identified and records made and sent to various headquarters to be sent back to the States. The War Department then was responsible to notify the next of kin.

The Margraten Cemetery in Holland was the burial place for these heroes. There were white crosses at each grave site identifying these soldiers. This was the final resting place for most of these forgotten heroes.

Some were returned to the States upon request of their families. Some were eventually moved to military cemeteries for their final resting place.

THE UNITED STATES ARMY WAS RUN BY MILITARY REGULATIONS

The United States Army was governed by Army Regulations that covered every phase of military life. In order to keep up with changes that occurred, the Army published War Department Circulars that contained, among other things, changes in regulations. These changes were effective immediately unless otherwise noted. New pages were eventually printed and they would replace the older regulations. The regulations were kept in composition type note books that made it easy to replace pages to accommodate changes.

Army Regulations were numbered with certain series that identified various phases of the military. For instance, the 35 series covered anything that dealt with finances. The 600 series covered personnel matters. There were regulations for just about everything that could possibly happen.

Every Infantry Division had a Judge Advocate that conducted hearings and discussions on all legal matters that were brought before their court. The judge usually had a staff that consisted of one or two lawyers and necessary personnel to carry out the routine business of the military courts.

The Judge Advocate Generals Office reviewed all military trials. There were three types of military trials. The Summary Trial was held by the Company or Battery Commander. His authority was limited to punishment of a maximum of seven days. There was no other person with authority of the Summary Trial. The accused was normally the only other person involved in this trial. The Special Court was the next higher military court. It dealt with matters that were above the limits of the Summary Court. Usually a staff of three officers were appointed to be on the Special Court. The accused was authorized to have one officer as a defense lawyer. Any number of witnesses could be called to be questioned by the Special Court and defense lawyer. The General Court was the highest military court that could be called to try a case. They handled all cases that were beyond the jurisdiction of the Special Court. All results of the three military courts were reviewed by the next higher court. The Commanding General had the authority to reduce the punishment assessed by the various courts.

All the above information was based on my memory of the rules and regulations in effect during the World War II years. Since it has been about 55 years since World War II, it is highly unlikely that these same rules and regulations are still in effect. They were appropriate during that time but things change.

The military also has a table of organization and equipment usually referred to as the TO&E. The table of organization lists the number of each rank in every organization. For instance, there are X number of Privates, Private First Class, Corporals, Sergeants, Staff Sergeants, Technical Sergeants and Master Sergeants. These limits cannot be exceeded except by special permission of some higher headquarters, usually the Commanding General at the Division Headquarters. If you happened to be the best Private in the Army, there was no way your Company or Battery Commander could promote you to Private First Class if there were no vacancies. Your only chance of promotion was the death of a Private First Class or a transfer of a Private First Class out of your organization. Privates were not dying very fast. Your chances for a quick promotion were very slim. These conditions existed in an organization that was a regular army unit with a full quota of all ranks.

After World War II, there were several enlisted ranks added such as Technical Corporal, etc. Many of the older units lost a large number of persons with various enlisted ranks and the opportunities were much greater than before.

During World War II, many promotions were made because of the casualties in the various organizations. During combat it was not uncommon to have several promotions from Private First Class to Corporal etc., to be made at one time. It was up to the Company Commander to send in the necessary information to the Battalion or Regimental Commander. There were many delays for these promotions because of the battle conditions that existed. It was up to the Company Commander to get this information to the proper headquarters at the earliest possible date. The primary concern of everyone was self preservation.

There was another regulation (GPLD) that had to do with the equipment you were issued. You were charged with the safe keeping of all your clothing and military equipment. The rule pertaining to government property lost or destroyed was one thing that you become familiar with early in your career. You had to pay for anything you damaged or destroyed. During combat it was not unusual to have some of your equipment damaged or destroyed. All you had to do was fill out a form giving details of your equipment that was damaged or destroyed during combat. This was an opportunity to get replacements for items that you lost or misplaced during combat. You would very rarely be questioned about such items. When the war finally ended, you had to take better care of your equipment because you had to pay for all these lost items.

MORALE AND PATRIOTISM IN THE MILITARY

We rarely ever heard of celebrities coming to the area where we were located. We were in a combat area just inside the Holland-Germany border in November 1944, when a young actor was brought into our area. We were housed in a bombed out coal mine administration building. Would you believe that Mickey Rooney was allowed to come spend the night with our troops? There was no entertainment planned for the occasion. I'm surprised that the military would permit such a visit by a celebrity.

On this same day the Red Cross Coffee Wagon was brought into the area. I remember two women were serving hot coffee to the few troops that were available. They didn't stay long and I'm sure they were told to leave the area because of the possibility of getting hurt.

Our 102nd Infantry Division was assigned two Red Cross Representatives who were authorized to stay in the area with the troops. They were given the authority by the military to perform certain duties that they normally carried out in the States. If any of the troops had family problems that needed to be resolved, it was their duty to take care of these problems. They would send TWX (military telegrams) messages back home to local Red Cross Units where the soldiers families resided and would verify any emergency that existed. The Red Cross was the official communication representative for the military during peace time and war time.

Our Red Cross Representative was a lawyer who volunteered for this work since he felt like he had to contribute something to the war effort. He was past draft age and he didn't have to subject himself to this type of duty. All I can say is that he was very patriotic. There were many patriotic people who helped with the war effort. I doubt that the country will ever see a generation of people more patriotic than this generation that lived during World War II.

The military was concerned about the welfare of our troops. The morale had a lot to do with the outcome of the drive into enemy held positions. Without high morale the troops could not accomplish their mission. Our commanders realized this and everything was done to keep morale at a high pitch. When General Eisenhower told the troops that they would have turkey for Thanksgiving, he knew that this certainly was a morale booster.

Every soldier in a combat area was given a ration of free cigarettes. This was another morale booster. The original ration was a pack a day. This didn't last long since the cigarettes were being stolen from the warehouses in Paris by the locals and probably by some GIs. Our ration was reduced to four packs per week and eventually the ration was practically eliminated since the looting and black marketing did away with most of the supply.

Looting became a big problem as our troops advanced further into Germany. As soon as the civilians left their homes, some of our troops would take whatever was handy. Our military would post signs "Looters will be shot" but that didn't scare off many troops. There wasn't much that you could carry so what was left of value would be picked up by the troops that would follow the original looters. To the victor belongs the spoils.

The infantry was usually the first to enter the towns that were conquered by our military. They had first choice of anything that was not damaged or destroyed. However, their mission in life was survival. The infantry losses were greater than any other losses by other units. Most of them could care less about looting. The pay of the privates was $30.00 a month. For some reason that I'm not familiar with, the military decided that all combat infantry men would be awarded the "Combat Infantry Badge." With this award, a pay raise of $6.00 a month was authorized.

I can assure you that the hazardous duty of a combat infantry man was worth 100 times the meager pay. Being patriotic had nothing to do with military pay. When you put your life on the line every day there is no price that can compensate for this duty. Many infantry men paid the supreme price to defend their country.

I hope our present generation will never have to serve in the military in some future war. Man has devised weapons that can destroy large areas of the countries of the world with one massive detonation of atomic or other weapons from a distance half way around the world. This is what our future holds in store for us. It takes only one "madman" like Hitler to destroy our world as we know it today.

RAW RECRUITS BECOME SOLDIERS IN THE HEAT OF BATTLE

After about two months in combat in Germany with the 380th Field Artillery Battalion, we were scheduled to receive replacements. We sent one of our vehicles to Brussels to pick up our replacements. After interviewing these new recruits, we found out that they were flown in from a training center in New York. These men had four weeks of basic training in the States which consisted of lectures on military discipline, the basics of marching and other military routines. They had very little information on weapons and did not have any opportunity to fire any kind of weapons.

The first thing we had to do was issue carbines to these raw recruits and find a place to test fire their weapons. Since there were coal mines in the area, it was not difficult to locate huge slag piles that were ideal places to set up our targets. I'm sure these replacements felt like they faced a new world since only yesterday they were enjoying the bright lights of New York.

I remember when I was drafted in January 1941, we spent the day in Pittsburgh going through all sorts of medical examinations. We were given meal tickets for lunch and supper which we used to buy our meals at a restaurant nearby. After the evening meal, we were told that we would be going to an induction center in Maryland that evening.

We didn't have an opportunity to go home to get any clothes and other essentials or visit our families. We did have a few minutes to call home, if you were lucky enough to get to a phone. Since we were one of the first draftees, things were not organized at all. We were treated like cattle rushing round half naked in the old courthouse building during our physicals.

After an overnight train ride, we arrived at the induction center in Maryland. The next three days were spent taking all sorts of aptitude tests to determine where our civilian experiences could be best used in the military. The fourth morning we lined up in the freezing weather to listen to the instructions regarding our assignment to our military installation. Each man on the roster was assigned to the same organization, the 2nd Infantry Division Training Center near San Antonio, Texas. Everyone of the 60-70 men would be assigned and trained as infantrymen regardless if you had a master's degree in education or five years experience as a boiler maker.

After 12 weeks of training, we were assigned to various infantry companies in the 23rd Infantry Regiment, 2nd Infantry Division. This was one of the oldest army units in the military and most of the men had at least a three year hitch completed. No vacancies existed for promotion since all the authorized quotas were filled. The table of organization authorized a certain number of non-commission officers in the enlisted ranks and no promotions could be made unless someone was transferred out or someone died.

Our infantry training was more or less routine from day to day. Calisthenics after breakfast for about 30 minutes, lectures on military customs and history of your particular organization and current events, practice of marching and getting familiar with the various marching commands, hiking about 10 miles with pack and other military gear except when weather conditions were too severe, learning to assemble and disassemble your rifle and pistol. There were other various military disciplines that were taught by non-commissioned enlisted men and commissioned officer personnel.

We were given specialized training in bayonet drill by a Sergeant Bronkhurst. He was the personal representative of General Kreuger who was the commander of the 8th service command. A mock-up of an enemy soldier was made up of a square bale of hay with enough wooden framework to support the hay. We were taught to fix bayonets (mounted on your rifle) and charge the enemy at full speed.

Your bayonet had to pierce through the entire bale to claim a casualty. If you didn't apply enough force, your efforts were not considered adequate to kill the enemy. According to Sergeant Bronkhurst, it was a matter of life or death in actual combat conditions. The sergeant could growl as loud and mean as a wild animal. If you didn't make it the first try, you would have to repeat until you did and I can assure you that you gave it your best shot the first time.

We got all this training for months and we still didn't go to the firing range to fire our weapons. It was nine months before we were finally taken to the firing range to use live ammunition in our rifles and pistols. Our targets were located at 200 yards and 300 yards and it was difficult to hit the bull's eye because of severe wind conditions and inclement weather with temperatures in the 30s. It seems to me that the military needs to schedule firing of weapons, especially raw recruits who have never fired a weapon, during more moderate weather conditions.

Months after the initial draft, the military still didn't give the raw recruits training in firing weapons before sending them to a combat zone as replacements. There certainly needs to be more serious thought given to this problem. Fortunately, your buddy would give you all the help he could to make an efficient soldier out of you. Life time friendships were made in fox holes and they were the best morale booster available.

I REMEMBER MY VISITS TO PARIS

My first glimpse of Paris was in September 1944. I was riding in a jeep with my battalion commander trying to establish a route for our Red Ball Express duty. Our battalion was given the order to prepare our unit to haul supplies from the port at Cherbourg to Paris. Paris had been liberated a few weeks but we still heard rifle shots coming from an area some distance from Paris proper. Paris was in a "brown out" situation and there was little to see as we entered the town after the hours of darkness.

We rode around Paris until almost day break and we stopped at some military headquarters to get some information regarding the routing of our trucks to the proposed warehouse area. After waiting for a couple hours we managed to talk to one of the officers who just got out of bed about 5:00 a.m. He wasn't too interested in helping us locate a route to the military warehouse in Paris.

Colonel Hannigan, our battalion commander, a West Point Graduate, had studied in Paris several years before and could speak French. He talked to several local folks while we were trying to find an appropriate route (one way) back to Cherbourg. The only people we found at this early hour in the morning were elderly men trying to find their way home after a night on the town.

With map in hand we finally managed to locate an appropriate route for our return trip to the port. We also located a midpoint where we would set up our headquarters and also a rest stop for our drivers who would stop every 3-4 days to rest and change clothes.

The next trip I made was about the first of November. We were relieved of our Red Ball Express duty and given orders to proceed to the Holland-German border of the famed Siegfried Line. While we were getting ready to move, it was determined that three of our men were missing. I received orders from Colonel Hannigan to go to Paris and check with the Military Police Headquarters to see if these men were incarcerated. We finally managed to find the Central Military Police Office and after going through the roster we located the names of our missing men. We were told that they were located in an old military prison on the outskirts of Paris. After some hours of driving, we found the prison and went in to inquire about our missing men. After some discussion these men were released since the prison personnel were told that we were headed for the front. We never did get all the facts about their imprisonment, all we knew was that these men were glad to get back to their batteries. We didn't get to see much of Paris because we were on a very tight schedule to get back to our battalion.

After our unit had seen combat for a few weeks and there seemed to be a lull in the fighting there were opportunities to get a couple days off to go to Paris. I managed to get on the list with several others from my battery. We started out traveling in GI 2-1/2 ton trucks for several miles until we got to a town in Belgium. Then we boarded a train to Paris.

We arrived in Paris about dark and checked in to a hotel that the military had acquired for housing our troops on these short vacations. It was a very old hotel with one rest room on each floor. Nothing fancy but it served the purpose.

Our meals were also served in the dining area of this hotel. Nothing fancy, just GI food prepared by our cooks with the help of some local chefs. The waiters were local French folks who had to be bribed to get an adequate amount of food for your meal.

Music was played during the evening meal by some fairly talented musicians who probably were members of the local symphony. It was a real treat to be entertained during our evening meal. I'm sure these musicians were well paid by our military. Meals were served for these musicians and since food was scarce, it was worth more than the fee for their services.

We spent our time observing the crowds of people traveling up and down the Champs Elysess, which was the famous street in Paris. There were thousands of folks riding bicycles up and down this main thoroughfare. Most of these bicycles were loaded with all sorts of supplies. It was not unusual to see six to 10 loaves of bread tied in a bundle on the back of the bicycle. Some carried stacks of wood that must have weighed 100 pounds. The bike riders were mostly elderly men and women. It seems like there was a constant flow of bike traffic all day and night.

There were many historical sights on or near the Champs Elysess. We didn't have an opportunity to visit any of the famous historical places but we did observe them from the sidewalk as we walked along this famous street. We did see the Eiffel Tower and Arc De Triomphe during our visit in Paris.

We managed to see the Follies by riding the subway a couple miles from our hotel. I don't remember paying any fee to get into the place. I guess our military uniforms got us in without paying a fee.

Something unusual I remember, we had to pay two Francs to enter the rest room. They must have been really hurting financially to have to resort to this type of action.

We didn't do anything exciting while in Paris but it still felt great to get away from the combat area for a few days.

FROM NEW YORK HARBOR TO FRANCE DURING WORLD WAR II

When I was a teenager, I remember the advertisements on billboards that were being promoted by the various military services. Join the Navy and see the world - Uncle Sam needs YOU - Join the Army - Join the Air Force - and Join the Marines. I think most teenagers thought about joining the various services but most parents were not all that enthused. The teenagers fell in love with the uniforms.

Some years later, I found myself on a ship headed for Europe and World War II. I was a member of the 380th Field Artillery, 102nd Infantry Division. We were in a convoy of several ships carrying soldiers from the 102nd Infantry Division and some other units. There were several merchant ships carrying supplies and military equipment in this convoy. These ships were located on our flanks and we could see them bouncing up and down in the rough seas. The Navy had three or four Corvetts about 20 miles in front of our convoy to protect us from the German warships. There were other Navy warships on our flanks that protected us from German submarines.

About two days out of New York Harbor, submarines were sighted and our Navy dropped depth charges (we called them ash cans) to destroy these submarines. We don't know if they hit their target because all we saw was a geyser that erupted out of the ocean and reached a height of about a hundred feet. That night about 9:00 p.m. an urgent call came over the loudspeaker for everyone to grab their life jackets and standby for further orders. This certainly was a frightening experience waiting for orders to abandon ship. With 5,000 men on this ship which was designed to carry about 500 tourists, you can imagine how terrifying this was. There were about 10 life boats on this ship that probably could accommodate the ship's crew. Thank God, the all clear message came about an hour after the original order was received.

During the day our convoy continued east without any unusual incidents. At night the convoy changed directions (zigzagging) several times. We don't know if this maneuver was planned or was brought about by the sonar sighting of enemy submarines by our Navy. Many of our merchant ships were lost at sea when they traveled without the protection of our Navy.

It took us 10 days to cross the Atlantic and we anchored at Weymouth, England overnight. The harbor was protected by submarine netting to keep German submarines from slipping into the harbor. We left Weymouth, England September 23, 1944, and arrived at Cherbourg that afternoon. Our ship was the *John Ericcson*, which was a cruise ship that was put into service during World War II to carry troops from the United States to France. There were five other ships in our convoy carrying troops across the Atlantic. A 10 day trip in a crowded ship crossing the Atlantic is not my idea of the kind of cruise that I would like to take again.

The *Queen Mary* was one of the most modern cruise ships available during World War II. The *Queen* was used to transport our troops from the United States to England. It could make the trip in three days and could outrun anything that the Germans had in their arsenal. The Queen was designed to accommodate about 3,000 tourists but it carried 30,000 soldiers from the United States to England. There were fortunes made by all cruise lines that transported our soldiers to England and France.

Feeding of our troops during the trip was a monumental task. Each soldier was issued a ration card which came in various colors. The holder of the blue card was to line up at 5:00 a.m. for breakfast then the red card holders would eat at 6:00 a.m. and the green card holders would line up at 7:00 a.m. Because of space limitations, there were no chairs or tables in the dining areas. A make shift table nailed to the wall (about a foot wide) was the nearest thing to a table that you could use to set your food on.

The noon meal consisted of soup and crackers one day and tea and cookies the next day. Dining room orderlies were picked from the duty roster. It was their job to go to the mess hall (I think there were several) and get the food. I remember the container that was used by the cooks to make soup. It was as large as a ladle that is used in the steel mills to make steel. The dimensions, as I remember them, were about six feet across and about seven feet deep. It was set about three feet off the floor. There were about six faucets near the bottom of the ladle. The cooks had a step ladder to climb so that the soup could be stirred and ingredients added. The cooks used an oar (probably taken from the life boats) to stir the soup. It was a real challenge to feed 5,000 troops from a ship designed to feed 500 tourists.

Everyone had some duty to perform during the 10 day trip across the Atlantic. Some of the men wouldn't eat lunch because they didn't like the English pea soup or the tea and cookies and they didn't want to stand in the long chow lines.

Most of the men laid on the deck and read books that were furnished by the Red Cross before we left the States. Some of the guys played cards all day to pass the time. Most of the guys in the "hold" came up on deck to get away from the stinking heat. Some of the men got sea-sick and had to get on deck to get some fresh air. The men slept on hammocks about four deep.

No one was allowed on deck at night. Black out conditions existed. Some of the card games and crap games were continued below deck after dark. Some of the men just worried about their families.

We all had plenty of idle time and that affected several of the men. We would wonder what was in the plans for us. How would we react when we got into combat? Would we have a chance to live through all the horrors of war? Many of our buddies didn't make it. I thank God that I made it.

THE SZALAY FAMILY

Jeffrey and Michael Nolan, grandsons, 1987.

Home from the war, with wife.

Parker Scott Nolan, great grandson.

Jeff, Lea and Parker Nolan, Sept. 2001.

Joe with wife Marie.

INDEX

Printed in the USA
CPSIA information can be obtained
at www.ICGtesting.com
JSHW022340140824
68134JS00019B/1598